CHRISTIAN HEROES: THEN & NOW

BROTHER ANDREW

God's Secret Agent

CHRISTIAN HEROES: THEN & NOW

BROTHER ANDREW

God's Secret Agent

JANET & GEOFF BENGE

YWAM PUBLISHING
P.O. BOX 55787 SEATTLE, WA 98155

YWAM), an international missionary organization of Christians from many denominations dedicated to presenting Jesus Christ to this generation. To this end, YWAM has focused its efforts in three main areas: (1) training and equipping believers for their part in fulfilling the Great Commission (Matthew 28:19), (2) personal evangelism, and (3) mercy ministry (medical and relief work).

For a free catalog of books and materials, call (425) 771-1153 or (800) 922-2143. Visit us online at www.ywampublishing.com.

Brother Andrew: God's Secret Agent

Published by YWAM Publishing
a ministry of Youth With A Mission
P.O. Box 55787, Seattle, WA 98155-0787

Sixth printing 2023

Library of Congress Cataloging-in-Publication Data

Benge, Janet, 1958–
Brother Andrew : God's secret agent / Janet and Geoff Benge.
p. cm. — (Christian heroes, then & now)
Includes bibliographical references.
ISBN 978-1-57658-355-5
1. Andrew, Brother. 2. Bible—Publication and distribution—Europe, Eastern. 3. Missions—Europe, Eastern. 4. Missionaries—Europe, Eastern—Biography. 5. Missionaries—Netherlands—Biography. I. Benge, Geoff, 1954– II. Title. III. Series.
BV2372.A7B46 2005
266′.0092—dc22 2005023019

ISBN 978-1-57658-355-5 (paperback)
ISBN 978-1-57658-578-8 (e-book)

Printed in the United States of America.

CHRISTIAN HEROES: THEN & NOW

Adoniram Judson
Albert Schweitzer
Amy Carmichael
Betty Greene
Brother Andrew
Cameron Townsend
Charles Mulli
Clarence Jones
Corrie ten Boom
Count Zinzendorf
C. S. Lewis
C. T. Studd
David Bussau
David Livingstone
Dietrich Bonhoeffer
D. L. Moody
Elisabeth Elliot
Eric Liddell
Florence Young
Francis Asbury
George Müller
Gladys Aylward
Helen Roseveare
Hudson Taylor
Ida Scudder
Isobel Kuhn
Jacob DeShazer
Jim Elliot
John Flynn
John Newton
John Wesley
John Williams
Jonathan Goforth
Klaus-Dieter John
Lillian Trasher
Loren Cunningham
Lottie Moon
Mary Slessor
Mildred Cable
Nate Saint
Norman Grubb
Paul Brand
Rachel Saint
Richard Wurmbrand
Rowland Bingham
Samuel Zwemer
Sundar Singh
Wilfred Grenfell
William Booth
William Carey

Available in paperback, e-book, and audiobook formats.Unit study curriculum guides are available for select biographies.

www.YWAMpublishing.com

Europe

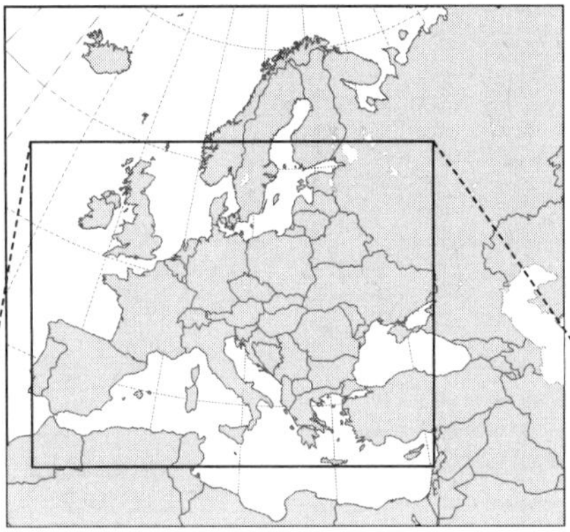

Central Europe 1950 to 1990

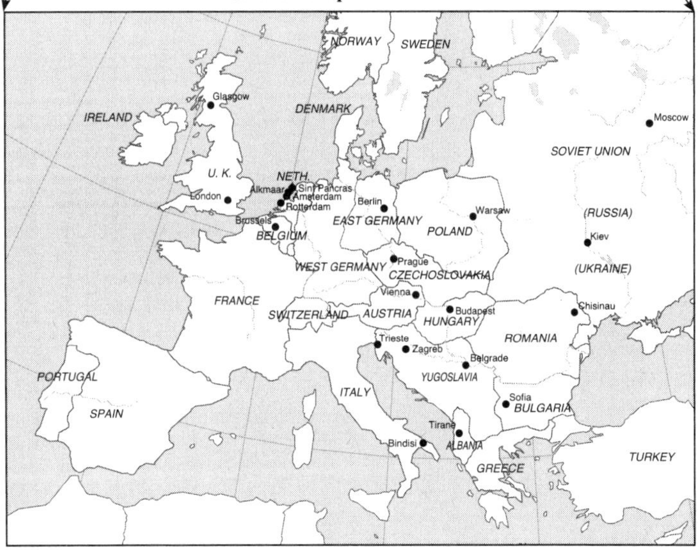

Contents

1. At the Border 11
2. Pretend Spy 15
3. Something Sinister Was Creeping over Europe 25
4. Resistance 37
5. Sure That He Had Found His Future 49
6. A Searing Image 63
7. Home at Last 73
8. Letting Go of Himself 85
9. Headed for an Unknown Adventure 97
10. An Experiment in Trusting God 107
11. Behind the Iron Curtain 121
12. The Cup of Suffering 137
13. "Don't Take No for an Answer!" 149
14. Someone to Share His Life With 161
15. Nerves of Steel 173
16. Into the Soviet Union 187
17. The Bamboo Curtain 199
18. The Fight Continues 209
Bibliography 217

Chapter 1

At the Border

Andrew pulled the car to a halt at the border. He had just crossed the Danube River from Bulgaria and was waiting to enter Romania. Four cars were stopped in front of him, and Andrew was relieved. *Surely it will take only a few minutes to get across the Romanian border,* he thought. He soon found out how wrong his assessment was. Forty minutes later the border guards were still inspecting the first car. When finally they waved that car on, the next car in line pulled up to the barrier. The guards then set to work inspecting it. An hour later everything inside the car had been meticulously spread out on the ground, along with the car seats and the hubcaps. The guards were now busy taking apart the engine.

Andrew stuffed his hands into his pockets and tried to look unfazed, though his heart was jumping through his chest. He had crossed the border into Communist countries numerous times before, but this was the first time he had seen anything like this.

What about my cargo—those precious Bibles! Andrew thought. If the guards stripped his car, they would be sure to find the contraband items. The Bibles would be taken from him, and he would end up in a Romanian prison, with no one from the outside knowing where he was. It was a heavy price to pay, but with God's help, Andrew hoped to smuggle the Bibles through right under the guards' watchful eyes.

Andrew did what he always did when facing such situations: he prayed silently about it. Then he did the exact opposite of what would seem to be the best chance of getting the Bibles over the border. Instead of keeping them hidden in the backseat of his car, he pulled out several of the Bibles and piled them beside him on the front seat, where the border guards would be sure to see them.

Finally, four hours after Andrew had pulled to a stop, a guard waved him forward. *Now is the time to stay cool, calm, and collected,* Andrew told himself as he drove his car up to the barrier. He smiled as he greeted the guards. "Nice day," he said pleasantly as he reached for his Dutch passport.

Being calm and collected under pressure was something Andrew knew how to do. As a boy growing up in Holland, he had learned how to face danger coolly and calmly, first in the form of a game he used to play to challenge himself and then, for real, actively opposing the Germans after they had invaded his country.

Chapter 2

Pretend Spy

Adventure! That was just what eight-year-old Andrew van der Bijl needed, and it was what he was missing. As he walked down the main street of the Dutch village of Sint Pancras, Andrew was overcome with how boring life was. He knew every house in the village and every family who lived in them. He knew what everyone did, or was supposed to do. It was 1936, and he assumed that twenty years from now he could walk down the same street and find that things were just the same. He imagined himself as a blacksmith like his father, going deaf from the constant banging of metal on metal and his skin pockmarked with burns from embers flying out of the furnace. He sighed. Where was the adventure he read about in library books? *In my imagination and nowhere else, that's where,* he told himself.

Andrew was halfway along the elm-tree-lined dike road when he decided to pretend that he was a spy creeping up on the Whetstras' house. He checked to see that no one was watching, and then he ducked behind a bush. Slowly he crept up to the window of the house. He had to step over a spare pane of glass that was propped against the house. He peered in the window and watched Mrs. Whetstra humming to herself as she put a tray of cookies into the woodstove.

Suddenly Andrew was struck with an idea. What if he climbed up on the roof and blocked the chimney with the pane of glass at his feet? How funny it would be to see the smoke billowing into the kitchen and Mrs. Whetstra trying to figure out what had happened. It would be funny, too, to see whether Mr. and Mrs. Whetstra got really angry once they discovered that their chimney had been deliberately blocked. Andrew had never seen a member of the Whetstra family frustrated or upset. The Whetstras were the Holy Rollers of the village, always reminding others to praise God when things went wrong. It would be interesting to see what *they* did when things went wrong. Why, they might even cuss!

With this happy thought in mind, Andrew grabbed the pane of glass and crept around to the side of the house to where a ladder lay against the wall. He slipped off his wooden clogs and started climbing the ladder, using one hand to steady himself and holding the glass pane in the other. At the top of the ladder, he transferred himself to the thatched roof of the Whetstra house, keeping a low profile and doing constant reconnaissance in case someone glanced up at him. Then he silently balanced the glass pane on top of the chimney. Immediately wisps of smoke began to collect under it.

Quickly Andrew climbed down the ladder and took up his former position behind the bush and waited. Mrs. Whetstra was no longer in the kitchen, but it was only a minute or two before she came rushing back. She took one look at the smoky room, let out a little scream, opened the oven door, and started fanning the oven with her apron. She looked so comical that it was all Andrew could do to stop himself from laughing out loud.

Mr. Whetstra soon bounded into the kitchen and peered at the stove. Then he spun around, ran out the door, and shot up the ladder. Andrew watched as he pulled the pane of glass from the chimney top and looked around. Andrew ducked low behind the bush. His heart raced. Had Mr. Whetstra seen him? He didn't think so. Balancing the glass pane in one hand, Mr. Whetstra climbed back down the ladder, set the glass where Andrew had found it, and went inside. Andrew heard him explaining to his wife what had happened as Mrs. Whetstra fanned the last few wisps of smoke out the window.

It was a confusing moment for Andrew, who had expected some show of anger, some flicker of frustration. Mr. and Mrs. Whetstra must have known that someone had put the glass on top of their chimney. Yet neither of them seemed concerned about the incident. Why was that? Andrew decided not to think about it anymore.

Since it was time to collect Bastian and bring him home for the evening, Andrew slipped out of his hiding place and continued along the dike road toward his home. Sure enough, his oldest brother Bastian, or Bas, as everyone called him, was standing by the third elm tree on the left. He stood there every day for hours on end, watching the people of the village go about their business. He never said a word to anyone. In fact, he couldn't speak at all. Although he was six years older than Andrew, he had to be treated like the baby of the family. It was easy for even a stranger to see that something was very wrong with Bas. Bas lived in his own little world, a world consisting of being dressed by his mother in the morning, standing under the elm tree during the day, and eating meals. But oddly enough, there was one thing that Bas could do better than anyone else in the family, or in the entire village for that matter. He could play music.

That evening, like every other evening after dinner, Andrew's father got up from the table, declared the meal to have been wonderful, settled himself at the pump organ, and began to play. Mr. van der Bijl did not seem to notice that his stiff, leathery fingers did not always hit the keys properly, and because he was partly deaf, he never seemed to notice whether he was playing too fast or too slow. In fact, sometimes his playing was so bad that Andrew wanted to put his hands over his ears.

While Mr. van der Bijl played, Bas would get down on the floor beside the organ and rest his head against the baseboard of the instrument. He would listen while his father tortured hymn after hymn on the keyboard. And then a strange thing would happen, something that amazed Andrew every time. Bas would crawl out from under the organ and tap his father on the shoulder. Mr. van der Bijl would slide off the organ stool, and Bas would take his place. As his hands floated across the keyboard and his feet worked the pedals, beautiful music would erupt from the organ. Bas played the same hymns his father had played, but this time they were played flawlessly and in perfect time. On warm summer evenings, it was not unusual for people from the village to gather outside the van der Bijl house and listen as Bas played the organ.

On the Sunday following the incident at the Whetstras' house, Andrew went to church with his family. He knew that attending church was the high point of his mother's week. Mrs. van der Bijl was not a well woman: she had high blood pressure and spent many hours each day sitting in front of the window. She always had the family's radio tuned to the gospel station at Hilversum, and Andrew was sure she turned it up extra loud when he was around to make sure that he could hear it from anywhere in the house. The gospel station drove him crazy, as did going to the Reformed church each Sunday. His only consolation was that he did not have to sit with his family during the service. Because of his father's deafness, the pastor had rigged up a special telephone-like device in the front pew for Mr. van der Bijl to use. But the short pew had only seven seating spaces, and since Andrew had three brothers and two sisters, there was not enough room for the whole family to sit in it.

Andrew would always eagerly volunteer to sit at the back of the church, and his mother would always thank him for the sacrifice he was making. But Andrew had a special reason for wanting to sit at the back of the church—he could easily slip out the door at the start of the service and slip back in before the service was over!

This Sunday was no different. As the congregation stood to sing the first hymn, Andrew slipped out of the church. During the winter he would run home, pull on his skates, and pass the time skating on the frozen canals. But today it was late spring, and the ice on the canals had long since melted. Instead Andrew headed for a nearby pasture, where several dairy cows were munching away on the lush, green grass. He flopped down in the grass a little ways from the cows and breathed in the scent of the flowering tulips and hyacinths while golden rays of sunshine spilled across his face. After several minutes of deep breathing and reveling in the sweet scent of the flowers, Andrew sat completely still. After Andrew had sat a few minutes like this, crows began to descend and perch on his shoulders. Sometimes they would try to peck his ears, and he would have to brush them off. But after a little while, the crows would come back and resume their stance on his shoulders.

Andrew seemed to have a sixth sense about when it was time for the church service to end. When he knew it was time to get back to the church, he would jump to his feet, the startled crows on his shoulders scattering into the air, and run as fast as he could toward the church.

Today, as usual, his timing was perfect, and Andrew arrived back at the church just as the last hymn was being sung. He waited patiently outside, and as the first members of the congregation emerged from the church he mingled with them. Then walking backward one step at a time, he reentered the church and found his parents. All the while he listened to the comments the parishioners were making about the sermon. Their comments might well be useful later on.

It was the custom in Holland for families to invite each other to their homes after church. The men would smoke thick cigars and drink even thicker coffee as they mulled over the morning's sermon. This particular morning Mr. van der Bijl had invited the Whetstras to the house.

Back at the house, Andrew felt a sense of exhilaration as the conversation began. He loved to see how far he could go in fooling everyone. To do this he used every snippet of conversation he had overheard at the end of the church service.

"So what did you think of the sermon, Andrew?" his father yelled at him. His father was always yelling because of his deafness.

"It was interesting," Andrew offered. Then he paused for dramatic effect. "But I think the pastor preached on Luke 3:16 last month. Perhaps he should teach something from the Old Testament for a change."

Andrew waited to see whether his father or Mr. Whetstra believed him.

"Yes, yes," Mr. Whetstra replied. "You are right, Andrew. It has been weeks since we have had a sermon from the Psalms. They are my favorite."

The conversation then took a turn, and Andrew waited for another opportunity to insert a word or two, confirming that he had paid attention throughout the entire church service.

After the ritual two cups of coffee, the Whetstras were ready to leave. Mr. and Mrs. Whetstra shook Andrew's parents' hands, and then Mr. Whetstra ruffled Andrew's hair. "It's good to see you concentrate on the sermon," he said. "Next time you pass our house, come in and visit with us. My wife makes the best cookies, and our stove is working flawlessly since I put in the new window pane."

Andrew felt the blood drain from his face. Was it a coincidence that Mr. Whetstra had mentioned cookies and how well his stove was working, or did he know that it was Andrew who had put the glass pane over the chimney? Finally Andrew decided that Mr. Whetstra knew that he had done it.

A long, uncomfortable moment passed as the Whetstras gathered their coats and headed out the door. Andrew knew that if Mr. Whetstra had said anything to his father about the incident, he would be whipped. His father was not a man to tolerate practical jokes, especially on unwitting neighbors. Andrew was thankful that Mr. Whetstra did not say anything more about the incident, and he very obligingly helped his older sister Maartje set the table for lunch after the Whetstras had left.

"Andrew," Maartje hissed as they worked together, "some people have the whole Bible in their heads but not one word of it in their hearts."

Andrew kept laying out the knives and spoons. He hated it when his older sister got like this. She was just as religious as his mother and was one more reason why he knew he would never live in Sint Pancras when he grew up. He would be moving on in search of real adventure out there somewhere.

Chapter 3

Something Sinister Was Creeping over Europe

It was the last day of May 1939, and in recent days a sense of gloom had settled over the van der Bijl house. Bas had somehow contracted tuberculosis, and the doctor had said that he could not hold on much longer.

Andrew was heartbroken. He had celebrated his eleventh birthday just three weeks before, but with his older brother lying deathly ill in his parents' bedroom, the celebration had been no fun. To make matters worse, only Andrew's parents entered the bedroom to visit Bas and care for him. Since tuberculosis was a very contagious disease, everyone in the house was taking a risk being there, and Mr. and Mrs. van der Bijl wanted to reduce as much as possible the risk of their other children's catching the disease. But Andrew did not care. In fact, he wanted to catch tuberculosis. He had decided that it would be easier to suffer with Bas and share in his fate than go on living after his brother had died. So one day while his father was at work and his mother sat beside her beloved radio, Andrew quietly opened the door to his parents' bedroom and slipped inside, shutting the door behind him.

Lying on the big bed in the bedroom was Bas, though Andrew hardly recognized him. The outline of his bones showed through the blanket, and his eyes were sunken. Andrew climbed up on the bed and lay down beside his brother. He put his arm around him and cradled his head. He felt hot tears streaming down his face as he kissed Bas over and over.

For the next two weeks Andrew waited expectantly to feel tightness in his chest or experience coughing fits, but nothing happened. He stayed as healthy as ever, while behind the bedroom door Bas continued to grow weaker. Finally, one morning in early July, Mrs. van der Bijl emerged from the bedroom, sobbing—seventeen-year-old Bas was dead.

The funeral service for Bas was subdued, partly because everyone felt sorry for his short and strange life and partly because something sinister was creeping over Europe. No one liked to talk about it much, but Germany, under the leadership of Adolf Hitler and his Nazi party, had become more and more aggressive toward her neighbors over the years. Finally, in March 1939, German troops had marched into Prague, Czechoslovakia, and had taken control of the place. Now the Germans were making territorial demands on Poland.

Normally Andrew would have been very interested in such events, but he had been so caught up in his brother's illness that he had hardly noticed the changes going on in Europe. Then, less than two months after Bas's funeral, the Germans invaded Poland. Two days later Britain and France demanded that the Germans withdraw their troops from the country. When the Germans did not withdraw, the British and French declared war on Germany. But the declaration of war did nothing to slow down the German advance. Within days the Germans' superior military force had smashed the Polish army.

With this happening to Germany's neighbors to the east, people in Holland began to wonder what might be in store for Germany's western neighbors. During World War I Holland had prided itself on remaining neutral, but people were beginning to wonder whether that would be possible this time around. They could not ignore the fact that the Germans seemed to show little regard for treaties or the neutrality of countries, and it seemed unlikely that the Germans would make an exception for Holland.

Then one night, soon after the Nazis had invaded Poland, Andrew sat by the radio with the rest of his family, listening to the latest news. Andrew heard the startling news that all reserve units of the Dutch army were being activated and that all privately owned motorcars were to be turned over to the government for its use. This was stunning information, and everyone, including Andrew, knew that it would not be long before the Dutch would be forced to fight the Germans.

Day after day Andrew stood under Bas's elm tree and watched the traffic. It seemed like everyone in Holland was on the move. Cars zoomed north and south, and large trucks carrying troops thundered by. Andrew wished that he were old enough to be a soldier in one of the trucks—that would be a real adventure. But he was only eleven years old and had to resign himself to following the progress of the war by listening to the radio.

The war soon drew closer than Andrew could have imagined. In April 1940 the Germans invaded Denmark and Norway under the guise of protecting these two countries from Britain and France. People in Holland knew that it was now only a matter of time before German troops marched into their country. The Dutch government decided that something needed to be done to slow down any German advance into Holland. It decided that one of the ways to do this was to destroy the polder lands. The polder was the name given to the low-lying land that had been reclaimed from the sea and was kept dry by dikes. Much of the land to the northeast of Sint Pancras had been reclaimed from the sea and was known as the Wieringermeer Polder. Andrew climbed to the top of the roof of the van der Bijl house to try to catch a glimpse of the dikes being destroyed. He did not see much, but he could hear the huge explosions as Dutch troops blew up the dikes.

Once it would have been Andrew's fantasy to see such explosions, but the results of blowing up the dikes was no fun for him. All of the people who lived on the Wieringermeer Polder streamed into Sint Pancras as their land was flooded. Every home in the village except the van der Bijls' housed a refugee family. Since the van der Bijl house was the smallest in the village and the family was one of the largest, the house had no room for another family. Andrew's mother compensated for not being able to take in a refugee family by cooking night and day. The soup pot was continually on the stove, preparing food to help feed the refugee families. Andrew's job was to peel endless amount of potatoes, carrots, and onions to go into the pot. There was never enough food for everyone who had sought refuge in the village, and for the first time in his life, Andrew would leave the table after a meal without feeling full. But he knew better than to complain about the situation; everyone was stretched to the limit.

Flooding the polders did not stop the German army's eventual advance into Holland. The Germans did not initially come on foot overland, as the Dutch had predicted, but came by air. On the night of May 9, 1940, Holland's prime minister addressed the nation by radio, trying to reassure Dutch citizens that Holland was still neutral. Andrew, like everyone else in Holland, wanted to believe the prime minister's words, but the words seemed hollow, given all that was happening across Europe. Andrew was still thinking about Holland's fate as he drifted off to sleep that night.

In the early hours of the morning of May 10, Andrew was awakened from his sleep by what sounded like a thunderstorm in the distance. He listened to the booming for several minutes, and then he heard another noise—the voice of someone yelling outside.

"It is not thunder," the voice yelled. "It's bombs. The Germans are invading!"

Andrew's heart thumped as he climbed out of bed. The rest of the family was up as well, and they all gathered around the radio, trying to hear news of what was happening in the country. They tuned to a radio station in London that confirmed that the Germans had indeed begun their assault not only on Holland but also on neighboring Belgium and Luxembourg. German planes were bombing airports all over Holland, and German paratroopers had begun parachuting into the country. The matter-of-fact voice on the radio from London noted that the Dutch were hopelessly outnumbered by the Germans, and it would be only a matter of time before German tanks began rolling over the eastern border into Holland.

When the sun came up, the stunned residents of Sint Pancras stumbled out into the streets to discuss the situation in the country. Suddenly airplanes—German planes—appeared overhead! The residents fled back indoors, and moments later the explosions began. The van der Bijl family huddled together as their house vibrated to the percussion of the blasts.

"The Germans are attacking the airfield," Andrew's father said in his booming voice.

Halfway between Sint Pancras and the town of Alkmaar, located five miles to the south, was a small military airfield. When the bombing was over, the German warplanes had reduced the place to a pile of rubble.

The airfield was not the only place in Holland to be reduced to rubble. Four days later, frustrated by the stubborn Dutch resistance, the Germans launched a massive bombing assault on the city of Rotterdam. They bombed the city mercilessly, destroying most of it. Adolf Hitler then threatened to do the same to the city of Utrecht if the Dutch did not surrender. On May 14, the Dutch prime minister surrendered the country to the Germans. It was a sad day for the Dutch and for the van der Bijl family. The only good news was that Queen Wilhelmina of Holland had managed to escape to London the day before the surrender.

With the surrender, German soldiers goose-stepped into Amsterdam while German tanks began crossing the border into the country. The occupation of Holland was complete, and it was not long before a radio announcer speaking in Dutch with a heavy German accent declared, "The German army is here to assist Holland. You are now part of the glorious Third Reich. We will keep you safe from the aggression of the French and British troops."

"Ha!" Andrew's father yelled when he heard the announcement.

A shiver went down Andrew's spine. All the German troops, tanks, and airplanes now in Holland did not make Andrew feel one bit safe. It was clear to him, and to everyone else, that the Germans, not the British or the French, were the aggressors.

That night, as he lay in bed trying to sleep, Andrew suddenly realized that his birthday had come and gone three days before on May 11. In the midst of the mayhem of the German invasion, Andrew, as well as the other members of his family, had completely forgotten it. Andrew was now twelve years old, old enough, he decided, to do his part in helping to run the Nazis out of his country. All his life he had wanted to go in search of a real adventure, and now one had come to him.

A week later a shiny, black car with swastikas on the front doors drove slowly past the van der Bijl house. Andrew followed the vehicle until it stopped in front of the mayor's house. A large man in a crisp, gray uniform stepped out of the car and walked straight into the house. A minute later the mayor emerged, looking flustered and carrying a suitcase. Another car pulled up, and four guards began carrying boxes from it into the mayor's house.

Andrew was astonished when he realized that the Nazis were in the process of setting up a local headquarters in the village. Within days of their arrival, subtle changes had taken place in Sint Pancras. The Nazis made a list of everyone in the village and then issued identity cards. Soon a pouch holding an identity card hung around Andrew's neck, and Andrew was forbidden to leave the house without it. Ration books were also handed out, to be used to buy food and essential items. To buy something, a person had to show his or her identity card and produce a ration coupon.

At first many residents in the village did not object too much to this system. After all, it helped keep things organized, and the Dutch like to have things organized. But slowly, one step at a time, the Nazis tightened their grip. A curfew was set in place. Everyone had to be inside by ten o'clock each night, and all the telephones in the village were to be handed in to the Nazis. Andrew's family was too poor to own a telephone and was not affected by this condition, but the lack of news did concern Andrew's mother and father. Dutch newspapers had to submit all of their articles to German scrutiny. Now the only reliable news came from Dutch newscasters who had fled to London and were broadcasting to Holland from there.

Listening to the news or anything else on the radio was soon banned. The Nazis announced that all radios must be delivered to the mayor's house. This demand caused quite a debate in Andrew's family. Andrew's mother's only entertainment was listening to radio concerts, and she did not see what business that was of the Nazis. In addition, his father liked to hear the news on the radio, or rather, have one of the children listen to it and then loudly relay the main events to him. Yet someone would pay dearly if the family were caught with a radio after it was supposed to have been handed in. Despite the danger, the family decided to keep the radio, which they moved up into a tiny crawl space at the back of the loft where Andrew slept. The floor in the crawl space was such a hodgepodge of different levels that it seemed unlikely that anyone would find the radio there. Each night one of the children was given the task of going up into the tiny crawl space and listening to the news on the radio. Afterward the child would relay to the rest of the family what he or she had heard.

Andrew suspected that many of their neighbors were doing the same thing, but no one talked about it. Everyone was too afraid of what might happen if the Nazis found out. It was impossible to tell who could be trusted anymore.

In mid-June the radio reported the ominous news that the Nazis had subdued France. German tanks and soldiers were rolling down the Champs-Elysées in Paris.

Soon afterward the situation in Holland changed for the worse. The Germans stopped claiming that they were in the country to help the Dutch. Instead they began using every Dutch resource they could get their hands on to keep the war going. Nothing was too small to escape their notice, not even Mr. van der Bijl's cabbages or the rubber inner tubes and tires on his bicycle. Andrew's schoolhouse became an army barracks, and classes were dismissed indefinitely.

Andrew, who was now a sixth grader, was not too concerned that school was canceled.

It was not long, however, before Andrew had extra work to do. The Germans went looking for teenage boys, as well as young and middle-aged men, to conscript into the military. No male in the village over the age of fifteen was safe, and that included Andrew's older brother Ben. Then one day Ben was gone. Andrew's mother explained that someone from the Dutch Resistance had come to escort Ben to a farm, where he could hide for the duration of the war. As a result, Andrew had to take over his brother's chores, including washing the family's clothes, since his mother was not strong enough to do it. As Andrew scrubbed and rinsed the clothes, his mind focused on one thing, and one thing only—how to become a part of the Dutch Resistance.

Chapter 4

Resistance

Andrew had quite a problem to grapple with. He was fairly certain that he would be considered too young to enter the Dutch Resistance unless he got their attention and admiration. But how?

The first scheme he came up with was to get his hands on some fireworks and create a commotion with them. Soon a plan formed in his mind. Alkmaar had a shop that had sold fireworks before the war, and Andrew thought that the owner probably still had some fireworks left. The question then was, what could he trade for fireworks? His father, who was an excellent gardener, had some tomatoes in the garden that the Germans had not yet taken. Andrew decided to take a basket of tomatoes into Alkmaar and see whether he could trade them for fireworks.

Before the war, Andrew would have borrowed his father's bicycle to make the five-mile trip to Alkmaar. By now, however, the Germans had confiscated all the bikes in the village, so Andrew had to walk the distance. He did not mind, though, since being out in the open helped him clear his mind. When he finally arrived in Alkmaar, Andrew was shocked at how different the place had become. Signs were posted in shop windows and doors that read "No Jews Allowed." And an anti-Jewish sign had been put up in the public park. An eerie feeling crept over Andrew, who was stunned at the way the Nazis had forced the normally tolerant Dutch people to accept their discrimination. It made him all the more determined to do what he could to help get the Germans and their hate-filled agenda out of Holland.

Andrew located the store that had formerly sold fireworks and stepped inside. "Do you still have any fireworks?" he asked politely.

The man behind the counter nodded and quickly disappeared into the rear of the store. He reemerged a few moments later. "This is all I have left," he said, placing a small box of run-of-the-mill fireworks on the counter.

Andrew looked at them. They were not exactly what he had wanted. There were no cherry bombs or other crackers that would make a big bang, but since they were all the man had, they would have to do.

"I have no money," Andrew declared, "but I

have these tomatoes." He lifted the basket he was carrying onto the counter.

The storekeeper picked up one of the tomatoes and squeezed it. "All right," he finally said. "You have a deal." With that the storekeeper removed the tomatoes from the basket and replaced them with the fireworks.

Andrew politely thanked the man and turned to leave the store. "Here," he heard the storekeeper say, and he turned back to look at him. In his hand the storekeeper held a cherry bomb. "It's the only one I have. Please take it."

"Thank you. Thank you very much," Andrew said as he reached out and took the cherry bomb, a broad smile spreading across his face as he did so.

"Now run along home," the storekeeper said. "You don't want to be out after curfew."

Andrew hurried out of the store and set out for Sint Pancras. Along the way he picked some flowers and laid them over the fireworks in the basket to disguise them.

At home Andrew hid the fireworks in the loft where he slept and waited for darkness to fall and his family to fall asleep. Soon the sound of snoring and rhythmic breathing told him the family was asleep. Andrew took the cherry bomb and slipped down the ladder from the loft, tiptoed across the floor, and disappeared out the front door of the house. He had to be careful; it was well after curfew. If the Germans caught him, he would be in real trouble, though he wasn't too concerned. He could run faster than anyone else in the village, including the Germans.

When Andrew was about to head over the small bridge that led to the dike road, he heard voices—German voices! A patrol was moving his way. Quickly Andrew slipped into the shadow of the house and pressed himself against the wall. One of the German soldiers shined his flashlight at the house, but the light did not illuminate the shadowy corner of the wall Andrew was standing against. Finally the patrol moved on down the road, and when they were gone, Andrew scurried across the bridge and ran as fast as he could in the direction of the mayor's house.

When he reached the mayor's house, Andrew positioned himself in the shadows and pulled out the cherry bomb. To increase the adventure of the moment, Andrew decided to wait until the patrol returned from the other end of the village. He did not have to wait long before he heard the crackle of the soldiers' boots on the road. He waited as the sound got closer and louder. His heart thumped in his chest as the patrol approached. Finally Andrew decided the time was right to light the cherry bomb. But as he was about to light the match, one of the German soldiers spotted him in the shadows and shined a flashlight on him.

"Halt," barked another of the soldiers.

By now the match had lit, and Andrew touched it to the fuse of the cherry bomb. The fuse began to glow orange as it lit, and Andrew decided it was time to run. He reminded himself that the advantage was his. He could run faster than these German soldiers, and he knew the village better than they did. But as he set out running, Andrew heard a sound he hadn't accounted for—the click of the bolt in one of the German rifles. It had not occurred to him that the Germans might shoot. All of a sudden he heard the crack of the rifle as its muzzle burst to life. The shot missed its target, and Andrew kept running as hard and fast as he could. Then there was a mighty explosion—the cherry bomb. Andrew wished he could have turned around to see his handiwork, but he had to get away. His life depended on it.

The blast diverted the soldiers' attention, giving Andrew the advantage. Andrew scurried across a small footbridge and dived into a patch of cabbages growing in a nearby yard. He held himself as close to the ground as possible. In the distance he could see the German soldiers looking for him. But he was well hidden in the darkness, and after an hour the soldiers gave up the search. Satisfied that he'd had enough adventure for one night, Andrew crept home and climbed back into his bed in the loft and fell asleep.

The next morning Andrew awoke feeling very pleased with himself. He headed outside to see whether anyone had heard the explosion in the night and was wondering what it could have been. On the dike road outside the van der Bijl house he encountered Mr. Whetstra.

"Good morning, Andrew," Mr. Whetstra greeted him. "I hear you went to Alkmaar yesterday. How was your trip?"

"It was fine," Andrew replied. "But Alkmaar is

different now. There are signs in store windows and in the park saying that no Jews are allowed."

"It is a sorry state of affairs, Andrew," Mr. Whetstra said. "But I hear things will soon get even worse for the Jews. The Germans are going to make them sew a large yellow Star of David on their clothing, with the word *Jood* [Jew] inside the star. This is a difficult time for them. Promise me you will pray for them, for all of us. Holland needs our prayers as never before, Andrew. You know that, don't you?"

Andrew nodded. He wasn't sure that God could do anything to help their situation, but he did not want to start a religious debate with Mr. Whetstra.

As daring as the episode with the cherry bomb had been, it did not satisfy Andrew. He had to think of something more useful than just annoying the Nazis with firecrackers. He soon came up with another plan. This time he would steal a Nazi gun and present it to someone in the Resistance. *That should help me get into the organization,* he told himself.

Andrew knew just where to find a German Luger pistol. As darkness was falling, he made his way to the home of a Dutch family who were collaborators. The man of the family served with the hated German SS. Andrew crept up to the window of the house and peered in. The man's green uniform, jackboots, and belt hung by the door. And there on the belt was his holster with the Luger tucked in it. Since nobody was in the room, Andrew sneaked around to the door and opened it. He stood still for a moment and listened. A radio was booming in the next room.

Probably a confiscated one! Andrew told himself. *The Nazis allow themselves privileges that we aren't allowed. I bet the whole family is in there, drinking good coffee and listening to the radio.*

When he decided it was safe, Andrew stepped inside the house. He was relieved that the volume of the radio would cover any noise he might make. Andrew reached behind the door for the holster and slid the pistol out. The gun felt cold in his hand, and he was aware that his heart was beating furiously.

As quickly as he had entered the house, Andrew left and began to sprint down the road toward his home. He was breathless by the time he crossed the small bridge into his yard. But he was also excited. He had done it! He had stolen a German Luger pistol, and he could hardly wait to hand it over to the Resistance.

Two days later Andrew's friend Kees told him about a Resistance cell meeting that was to be held in a nearby Christian primary school. Under the cloak of darkness, Andrew made his way to the location and knocked on the school door, using the secret code Kees had given him. A loft door swung open, and Andrew entered the world of the Dutch Resistance. His entrance fee to the meeting was the German pistol he had stolen. The meeting was already under way when Andrew arrived, and the eight or so young men were listening to Radio Orange, the Dutch Resistance radio station broadcast from London that Queen Wilhelmina had set up in exile.

As Andrew sat huddled with the others around the radio receiver, he felt a deep sense of contentment. At last he was one of them, the daring ones who were doing something to combat the dark cloud that had descended over Holland.

When the radio broadcast was over, the group discussed more ways to steal Nazi guns and bikes and how to counterfeit ration cards. Andrew also learned that the Resistance was helping many Dutch Jews who were secretly passing through Sint Pancras on their way to the coast, where they were picked up by boats and smuggled across the English Channel to Great Britain. It seemed that in the Dutch Resistance there was plenty of work for everyone, and Andrew soon found himself volunteering to disrupt Nazi transportation. He did not have the resources to blow up trucks or bridges, but Kees gave him instructions on how to ruin their car engines. This involved dumping sugar in the gas tank, which in turn would clog up the engine and cause it not to run.

The Resistance workers left the meeting one at a time, and when Andrew's time came to slip through the door and make his way across backyards to his home, he felt satisfied. He told himself that the German lieutenant's staff car was going to be the first gas tank to receive the "sugar treatment."

Two nights later Andrew was able to accomplish his mission with little difficulty. However, he did notice his mother's eyebrows raise when she went to refill the sugar bowl soon afterward. She said, "I hear some of the Nazis are having problems with their cars." A smile played around her mouth as she spoke, and Andrew knew he had her blessing to take the family's precious sugar ration for such a purpose.

Andrew continued with his Resistance activities, taking messages from one Resistance cell to another or escorting Jews to safe houses for the night. The stakes for involvement in such activities, however, grew increasingly high for Andrew and his coworkers. When, by 1942, the Nazis had dropped any pretense that they were in Holland to protect and liberate the Dutch, the ugly truth was there for everyone to see: the Nazis intended to take over all of Europe, and eventually the world, and their need for Dutch supplies and manpower had increased.

Soon the German lieutenant and his men who occupied the village were replaced by a much more odious group of German soldiers, known as the *razzia*. The razzia did not station themselves in the village but rather made raids on it. At any time of the day or night, Nazi trucks would roar into Sint Pancras, sealing off the route in and out of the place. Squads of machine-gun-toting soldiers would then jump out of the trucks and search every house. If radios or other banned items were found, the homeowner was marched off and handcuffed inside one of the trucks. Occasionally someone who annoyed the razzia would be shot on the spot.

The Germans were actually after able-bodied men. Andrew was fourteen years old now. He was lean and fit and just the kind of youth they were looking for. It became imperative for him and the other men of Sint Pancras to never let down their guard. Even when they slept, they did so with the window open and one ear listening for the rumble of truck engines in the distance.

Once the men heard the dreaded sound of approaching trucks, they had only a matter of minutes to head for safety—the safety of the swamp beside the railroad tracks. As the fastest runner in the village, Andrew always led the group as they ran for their lives across the flatland toward the dike on top of which the railway line sat. The men and boys would spread out among the swampy marshes at the foot of the dike and hide until the Germans left.

A year later, in 1943, the situation in Sint Pancras became even more desperate. The Nazis turned the electric power off to the village, making everything damp and gloomy. Food was desperately short—the last of the precious tulip bulbs had long since been eaten—and people scavenged for swamp weed to eat. Andrew was particularly distressed when the people of the village needed firewood so badly that they cut down first one, then two, then all of the elm trees that lined the dike road. He recalled how Bas had loved to stand under the elms and watch the world go by, but now he was almost glad that Bas was gone. The Nazis had rid Holland of the weak and infirm, and Bas would have been taken away and killed for sure. As it was, in their search for able-bodied men, the razzia were now after not only Andrew and his younger brother Cornelius but also Mr. van der Bijl, and they all had to dash to safety in the swamp when they heard the rumble of trucks in the distance.

After spending hours in the swamp hiding from the Germans, Andrew's father often coughed all night. Also, Andrew's mother was growing weaker each month, and there were times now when she stayed in bed all day. Andrew watched as she turned away food at the table so that others could eat. He wondered whether she would starve to death.

By now all of the excitement of being a member of the Resistance had drained away in the harsh light of Nazi oppression, and Andrew wondered whether the war would ever end.

Chapter 5

Sure That He Had Found His Future

At last the radio hidden in the narrow crawl space at the back of the loft began to offer some rays of hope. The Americans, who had joined the Allies in the war in December 1941, were apparently planning with the British to attack the Germans in occupied France. Fearing such an invasion, Hitler had sent a huge contingent of forces to the northwest coast of France to repel the Allied forces.

Days went by, then weeks, and everyone in Sint Pancras began to wonder whether the proposed invasion had just been a malicious rumor. Then in the summer of 1944, the balance of power began to shift in favor of the Allies. On June 6 the rumored invasion finally began. Allied forces stormed ashore on the beaches of Normandy on the north coast of France. By August they had taken back Paris!

Soon hundreds of Allied bombers were flying over Sint Pancras on their way to bomb Germany into submission. It was a tense time for Andrew and his family. While it seemed inevitable that the Allies would liberate Holland, everyone was aware of just how dangerous—and desperate—the Germans had become. The people in the village were all wondering the same thing: Would the Germans shoot everyone in the village as they retreated? And would Allied bombs meant for the Nazis also fall on them? They had no way of knowing for sure, and everyone waited tensely to see what would happen.

By February 1945 the Allies had taken back all of France and were positioned along the border of Germany, all the way from Holland, south of the Maas River, through Belgium and Luxembourg.

Then on May 1, 1945, the radio reported wonderful news: Adolf Hitler was dead. Four days later his successor surrendered Holland and ordered all Nazi troops to leave the country. Word quickly spread that Canadian soldiers had pushed into Alkmaar and that the Germans were hurriedly packing up their belongings and fleeing. Suddenly and unceremoniously, Sint Pancras was liberated!

When Andrew heard the news, he raced outside. People were weeping and celebrating in the street. But Andrew did not join them. He sprinted off to Alkmaar to find the Canadian liberators. When he got to Alkmaar, he begged for food for his mother.

A Canadian soldier told him to wait a moment. When he returned, he held a bag of bread crusts, which he handed to Andrew. As far as Andrew was concerned, the bread crusts might as well have been gold as he tucked the bag into his shirt and sprinted home to share the crusts of bread with his family.

Andrew was overwhelmed with emotion as he watched his mother eat a crust of bread. Tears streamed down his mother's cheeks as she ate. Andrew cheered himself with the news that soon everyone in Holland, including his mother, would have enough food to eat.

Two days later a strapping twenty-one-year-old strolled through the door of the van der Bijl house. It was Ben! No one had heard from him during the five years of the occupation, because it was not safe to pass along messages. Now here was Ben, standing in front of them all, once more making the van der Bijl family complete.

After the euphoria of the liberation of Holland and the end of the war wore off, it was time for the family to take a realistic look at what to do next. The younger children went back to school to try to catch up on all the learning they had missed. Andrew, however, did not know what to do with himself now, since he was too old to go back to sixth grade. He liked to run every day, and he helped his mother with work around the house, but he knew that eventually he would have to find a direction for his life.

Andrew's father was apparently thinking the same thing too, because one day during the summer of 1945 Andrew's sister Geltje met Andrew at the door with the news that their father wanted to see him in the garden. Mr. van der Bijl was tending the cabbages, and when he saw Andrew approaching, he straightened up and leaned on his hoe.

"You wanted to see me, Papa?" Andrew said, almost shouting.

"You are seventeen years old now, Andrew," Mr. van der Bijl boomed back.

A lump formed in Andrew's throat. The conversation he had been dreading was about to take place, right there in the cabbage patch and loudly enough for the neighbors to hear.

"Yes, sir," he replied.

"What are you going to do with your life?" his father asked.

Andrew did not know what to say. He had thought about the question himself, although nothing he thought of filled him with any sense of excitement. But he knew one thing for sure: he was not going to spend the rest of his life in boring, old Sint Pancras. Somehow he was going to see the world. But how would he tell his deaf, old father this?

"I will give you until fall to decide on a trade. Then I want an answer. Do you understand me?"

Andrew nodded. He understood his father well enough. But what could he do? He decided to clear his head by going for a run. As he jogged along the dike road and out onto the polder, he thought about what he did *not* want to do. He did not want to work indoors or in a garden or as a blacksmith, like his father. And he could not study further, because his education had gone only to the sixth grade, not that he wanted to study more anyway.

Andrew decided to approach the problem a different way. He asked himself what exactly he was good at. The answer came to him as he ran—*stealing guns, passing on secret messages, evading Nazis, and running like the wind*. But what good were those things now that the war was over? Then it struck Andrew. His thinking was far too small. The war might be over in Holland and the rest of Europe, but he had recently read how the Dutch army was having difficulty putting down a local uprising in the Dutch East Indies. Andrew's pace quickened as he tried to recall what he had read in the newspaper.

The Dutch East Indies, as Indonesia was then called, had been under Dutch control for three hundred years, until the Japanese occupied it during the war. Now that the Japanese were gone, some people in Indonesia wanted to be free of Dutch rule as well. Of course Andrew knew that this would never happen and that the Dutch army was sending recruits to the East Indies to subdue the rebels.

As Andrew ran, he pieced together a mental checklist of why he would make a good soldier. He was fit and young, and he was looking for adventure. On the negative side, he did not have much education. But he figured that many Dutch teenagers were in the same situation. He could hardly wait to get home and tell his family what he had decided to do.

Although Andrew's brothers and father were enthusiastic about his joining the army, his mother and sisters were not. Their reaction did not surprise Andrew, who knew that his mother wanted him to stay close to home.

The Whetstras did not think much of his decision either. "I will pray for you," Mr. Whetstra said. "I hope you find what you are looking for, Andrew."

Andrew did not really care what they thought. He was sure that he had found his future. He could see himself already, stationed on a tropical island, eating pineapples and drinking Javanese coffee.

Although Andrew applied to join the army right away, he was not allowed to sign up until his eighteenth birthday on May 11, 1946. The wait seemed interminable, but at last he was accepted and sent on his way to Gorkum, in the south of Holland, for training.

Andrew loved every bit of the training, from crawling around under camouflage nets to learning to fire semiautomatic weapons. It was just like being in the Resistance, only now he got paid for doing it. He also attracted a lot of female admirers, and Andrew made sure that everyone he met knew that he was training to be a soldier.

On Sundays he attended a local church, where each week he was invited to lunch by a different family. If the family had a pretty teenage girl, Andrew was sure to be extra charming and confident. "Naturally, with my talent, I'm being trained for hand-to-hand combat," he would tell people.

What he should have told the families who invited him to eat with them was that he was not really interested in the church service or their company. What he hoped for was that they would write to him and send care packages once he was deployed. On a visit to one family, he met a particularly attractive girl named Thile. Andrew decided she was the prettiest girl he had ever seen, with her jet-black hair and smooth, white skin. He made a note to himself to write to her in the first batch of letters he sent out from Indonesia.

Finally the training came to an end, and in November 1946 Andrew went home to say goodbye to his family. He felt proud wearing his crisp new uniform with its shiny brass buckle. Despite the new uniform and training, Andrew's mother was not impressed. "Why do you always think about killing?" she asked him.

Andrew did not have a definitive answer to her question. He had lived in the midst of war since he was twelve years old, and now uniforms, guns, and combat all seemed normal to him.

Just before Andrew left for Amsterdam to join his army unit, his mother reached into her apron pocket. "Here, son, I want you to take this with you," she said.

Andrew's heart sank. Andrew's mother was giving him her personal Bible. Andrew had hoped to get out of the house without any religious literature.

"Just promise me you will read it," Mrs. van der Bijl went on.

Andrew decided not to argue. He mumbled a thank you and pushed the Bible down to the bottom of his duffel bag. As far as he was concerned, it could stay there until he got back.

After Andrew joined his unit, the men were loaded aboard the transport ship *Sibajak* for the trip to the East Indies. As the ship made its way to Southeast Asia, Andrew wrote his first batch of letters home to his old and new friends. During the time of his training, he had managed to collect the names of seventy-two families, and he hoped that his letters to them would reap him a good harvest of care packages containing chocolates and cheeses.

At the top of Andrew's list of people to write to were Thile and her family. Andrew wrote to Thile about how he loved life at sea and how he could not wait to start serving his country by putting down the rebels. Like most of the letters that followed, this letter was filled with bravado and bluff. Andrew had little idea of what he was about to encounter in the Dutch East Indies.

The truth was that Andrew was not properly prepared to understand and embrace another culture. Sure, the Germans had invaded Sint Pancras, but they were Holland's European neighbors and not too distant culturally. But as he disembarked the *Sibajak* in Jakarta three days before Christmas, Andrew was introduced to an entirely different way of life.

The first thing Andrew had to get used to was the heat. It had been damp and foggy, with temperatures only in the forties, when he had boarded the transport ship in Holland. But now, as he disembarked, the temperature was twice that, and the humidity was stifling. As he lugged his large duffel bag down the gangplank, beads of sweat formed on his brow.

The Dutch influence on Jakarta was immediately obvious. The waterfront was lined with neat warehouses, beyond which sat brick houses with red tile roofs. The houses lined neat streets and squares, and canals seemed to be everywhere.

As Andrew made his way through the city with his fellow soldiers, the neat, Dutch-influenced part of the city gave way to a different Jakarta. The streets narrowed and seemed to branch off at odd angles, and they teemed with native people and activity. At the side of the road, people were selling all manner of things, from fruits and vegetables, some of which Andrew had never seen before, to spices, fabrics, and clothes. The streets were also clogged with *betjaks,* large, brightly painted tricycles that served as taxis. The betjaks ferried around dark-skinned people who bantered excitedly in the strangest language Andrew had ever heard. How different it all was from Sint Pancras.

Soon after arriving in Jakarta, Andrew was among a group of soldiers chosen to go to one of the 13,677 islands of Indonesia to undergo special commando training. During this time the trainees were briefed on their enemy. Their enemy was not everyday Indonesians but a group of rebel guerrillas called the PNI. The group, which was led by a man named Sukarno, was fighting to oust the Dutch from Indonesia. However, the guerrillas did not fight in a "European" way. Instead they mounted lightning-fast, hit-and-run attacks against the Dutch, who, even with their superior weapons, tanks, and cannons, found it hard to defend themselves. A growing group of Communist guerrillas were also harassing the Dutch. But despite the elusive nature of their enemy, Andrew loved every minute of his commando training in the tropical jungle. The training was grueling, but with his tall, sinewy body and his long-term endurance, Andrew began to feel that he could take on any challenge. But as he soon found out, he still needed to learn a few skills.

"Soldier, can you drive a Bren carrier?" an officer asked Andrew one day as he walked out of the company headquarters.

"Yes, sir," Andrew said with all the confidence he could muster.

"Then that one there needs to go to the motor pool for servicing. Let's go," the officer said, pointing to a nearby Bren carrier.

In truth Andrew had never driven one before, or any other motor vehicle, for that matter. But while he was being transported around in a carrier day after day during his training, Andrew had studied how the driver operated the vehicle and had come to the conclusion that it was not too difficult.

Bren carriers were large troop carriers mounted on tracks. They were halfway between a tank and a truck and seemed to be able to effortlessly glide over the most rugged terrain. Andrew climbed up into the driver's seat, with the officer seated beside him. He studied the dashboard, trying to familiarize himself with the controls. The key was in the ignition, so he turned it, and the Bren's engine throbbed to life. Now Andrew studied the pedals at his feet. Which one was the clutch? The first pedal he pushed went all the way to the floor. He decided that that was the clutch, and he slid the vehicle into gear. He hit the accelerator and pulled his foot off the clutch, as he had observed the driver do. Immediately the hulking vehicle jerked forward and began to gather speed. Andrew raced along the street, barely missing several soldiers crossing the road. The carrier went faster and faster, and when Andrew glanced at the officer sitting beside him, he saw that the officer's knuckles were white as he gripped the sides of his seat and that his legs were braced against the floor.

The motor pool building was quickly approaching. It was then that Andrew realized that he did not really know how to stop the vehicle. He felt a tingle of panic run through him. Even with his foot off the accelerator, the Bren carrier was barreling along. Without looking, Andrew plunged his foot down on what he supposed would be the brake. Unfortunately he hit not the brake but the accelerator. The troop carrier lunged forward even faster. Andrew pulled up his foot, but it was too late. The Bren carrier plowed into the back of a row of Bren carriers waiting to be serviced at the motor pool, causing them to concertina into one another. When the Bren carrier finally came to a halt, the officer beside Andrew jumped out, ashen-faced and shaking. Meanwhile a gruff sergeant pulled open the driver's door of the Bren and demanded to know what Andrew thought he was doing.

"Driving to the motor pool, sergeant," Andrew said.

The sergeant glared at Andrew.

His confidence shaken, Andrew thought fast. He pointed to the ashen-faced officer standing on the other side of the Bren carrier. "He asked me if I knew how to drive one of these. But he didn't ask me if I knew how to stop one!" he said.

The next morning Andrew needed all his confidence; he was being shipped out on a combat mission. His company was being sent to reinforce a company in which three-quarters of the men had been killed in the fighting. It was a sobering moment as Andrew tied his boots, slung his duffel bag over his shoulder, and reported for duty.

Andrew soon discovered that life on the front lines was very different from training. For one thing, the soldiers were no longer shooting at paper targets with their weapons but were shooting at real people. And despite what they had been told about how they were not fighting ordinary Indonesian people but were fighting Communists and PNI guerrillas, in the field it was hard to tell who was who. Any suspicious-looking person was likely to be shot on sight.

Andrew also learned that firepower was everything. Any unusual sound or situation was met with a hail of gunfire and a barrage of hand grenades. Andrew loved to feel the kick of his machine gun as clip after clip of ammunition burst from its muzzle. And afterward he would take pride in the damage his weapon had inflicted as he walked around dead bodies and destroyed villages. This was the excitement he had been looking for.

As the weeks rolled by, however, Andrew began to notice that his excitement was draining away, and a deep emptiness seemed to take its place. The flash of bullets exploding from the barrel of his gun no longer seemed to have the same hold over him. And Andrew began to feel a gnawing in the pit of his stomach when he saw the carnage that was being inflicted on the local people. Now when he returned to camp at night, Andrew found himself taking swig after swig of gin. The gin would burn his throat at first, but within an hour of swigging it, Andrew was numb to the day's events. And that felt good, very good.

Chapter 6

A Searing Image

Time on the battlefront passed slowly for Andrew. Although Andrew received regular letters from home, the little Dutch village of Sint Pancras seemed a million miles away. Like Andrew, most of the other soldiers in his company lived lives of quiet desperation as each week one or more of their comrades were killed or wounded in the fighting. The only glimmer of joy in Andrew's life was a three-foot-tall gibbon.

Andrew had been on leave in Jakarta when, as he walked through a market, he passed the gibbon. The ape was tethered to a pole and sat on top of it, peeling an orange. As Andrew passed by, the gibbon leapt off the pole onto Andrew's shoulder, where it held out a segment of the orange it had just peeled for him to eat. Andrew smiled, and the animal seemed to smile back at him. Andrew bought the ape and took him back to camp.

The gibbon was a hit with Andrew's fellow soldiers, who loved to pet and play with the animal. But Andrew noticed that sometimes when one of the other soldiers touched the gibbon near its waist, it often winced in pain. When he investigated, he discovered that the ape had something imbedded under its skin that caused the pain. Andrew took a razor and carefully cut into the gibbon's skin. He was amazed that the animal just lay there and let him cut. Andrew pulled the gibbon's flesh apart and discovered that the embedded object was a length of wire. Carefully he cut some more and then removed the wire. When the cut had healed, the gibbon never again winced in pain when someone touched its waist.

Having the wire removed seemed to bond the gibbon to Andrew. The two became inseparable. Sometimes Andrew would go running, with the gibbon clinging to his shoulders. At other times, especially at night when he had no one else to talk to, Andrew would sit and talk to his gibbon. He would tell the ape how he felt inside about the fighting going on around him. Somehow his conversations with the gibbon seemed to ease his conscience.

As the conflict dragged on, Andrew became recognized for his bravery and quick thinking on the battlefield. One day when he and his platoon were out on patrol, they came to a hill. Andrew sprinted off up the hill and was soon one hundred yards in front of the others, who were huffing and puffing their way up the side of the jungle-covered slope. But as he ran over the ridge at the top of the hill, Andrew came face-to-face with ten heavily armed guerrilla fighters. He was outnumbered and outgunned, and the rest of his platoon were still only halfway up the hill. Andrew thought fast; his life depended on it. He knew that if he opened fire on the guerrillas, they would fire back and he would be dead in seconds. The only way he could see out of the situation was to bluff the guerrillas. Instantaneously he raised his gun and pointed it at the guerrilla fighters. "The war is over for you," he said. "Drop your weapons. You're completely surrounded." He said it as forthrightly and as convincingly as he possibly could.

Andrew's heart throbbed in his chest as he waited to see what the fighters would do. To his relief—and amazement—the guerrillas threw down their weapons and surrendered. The bluff had worked, and his fellow platoon members were astounded when they finally stumbled over the ridge and discovered Andrew guarding ten prisoners at gunpoint.

One day an event occurred that Andrew could not even face talking about with his pet gibbon. The previous three weeks had been tense ones. Communist guerrillas had actively entered the conflict between the Dutch and the PNI. As a result, Andrew and his fellow soldiers were now fighting two different enemies. The fighting would have been much easier if the Communists and PNI fighters had fought in open warfare, but they preferred to plant land mines and set booby traps that could explode anytime and anywhere. The land mines in particular created much anxiety among the Dutch troops. One wrong step and a person could be blown to bits in a second.

On the day of the incident, Andrew was part of a squad marching through a peaceful village. The men were confident that no land mines were around, since the village was occupied with men, women, and children. Then *BOOM!* A deafening noise filled the air, and shrapnel fell like hail. The men had walked into a nest of land mines. Andrew turned his head just in time to see his friend Arnie blown apart by a land mine he had stepped on. The percussion from the blast threw Andrew to the ground. When he got up, Andrew was pulsing with rage. Surely the residents of the village knew of the location of the mines, or they would have stepped on them themselves. It seemed to Andrew that everyone else in the squad must have come to the same conclusion at the same time. Suddenly gunfire erupted all around him. It was as if the air had turned to molten lead, as frightened and angry Dutch soldiers opened fire with their rifles and machine guns, indiscriminately shooting at houses, people, animals, trees, anything that happened to be in their line of fire.

When the guns finally fell silent, the squad carefully made their way around the nest of mines and headed toward the edge of the village. All around them was destruction. The village was completely destroyed, and from the bodies strewn about, it seemed to Andrew that not a living thing had survived the onslaught. *But they deserved it,* Andrew rationalized. *They knew the mines were there. They should have said something. By not saying anything, they were as culpable as the guerrillas who had planted the mines.* Then he saw a sight that cut his rationalizing to shreds. On the ground in front of Andrew, lying in a pool of her own blood, was a young mother. Pressed at her breast was a baby. The mother and her child had been shot through with the same bullet.

What kind of animal have I become? Andrew asked himself as he stared at the mother and her baby. *How could I behave like this?* For an instant Andrew felt like putting his gun to his head and pulling the trigger. *Why? Why? Why?* All the killing suddenly seemed so pointless to him.

Andrew did everything he could think of to get the image of the dead mother and her baby out of his mind. He even went to talk to the company chaplain. But the chaplain tried to make a joke about the situation, and Andrew left feeling surer than ever that if there was a God, He was certainly not interested in a Dutch soldier on a tropical island in Southeast Asia.

The image of the dead mother and baby was burned so deeply into his consciousness that Andrew turned to the one thing he knew would fade the memory for short periods—alcohol. When he sat at the bar with his friends, Andrew drank twice as much as they did. It was only then, as the gin burned in his stomach and blurred his consciousness, that he could forget what he and the rest of the squad had done. But when the effect of the alcohol had worn off, Andrew would feel more worthless than ever.

Finally Andrew decided that he had nothing to live for, and he became the most daring soldier in the company. He reasoned that if he could not kill himself, the enemy could do it for him. He bought a bright yellow straw hat to wear when he was in combat, a beacon of his presence to anyone who wanted to shoot him. But somehow the enemy's bullets always missed.

In the midst of his despair, Andrew received crushing news from home. One day a letter from his brother Ben arrived, describing a funeral in the village. It was only after he had finished reading the letter that Andrew realized that Ben was talking about their mother's funeral. An earlier telegram informing Andrew of his mother's death had apparently not been delivered.

After reading the letter, Andrew decided to go for a run in the jungle to try to find some peace of mind. But it was useless. With every stride he took, he thought about his mother lying in a coffin, and then images of all the people he and his company had killed flooded his mind. Once again Andrew turned to alcohol to dull the pain.

Sometimes, between drinking bouts, Andrew wrote letters to some of the people he had met while in training at Gorkum. He told them about how he felt and about some of the things that had happened to him since he had left Holland. But the people he wrote to all wrote back with the same reply: "You are serving your country honorably and following orders, so don't let it trouble your conscience."

But it did trouble his conscience—deeply. Andrew started writing about his feelings to Thile, the girl with the white skin and beautiful black hair he had met in Gorkum. Thile did not dismiss him with glib words but wrote back, telling him about how God could forgive him and how he needed to forgive himself as well. Her letters made some sense to Andrew when he was sober, but when he was drunk, he thought Thile's advice to be simplistic and childish.

Once he even wrote a letter to Thile telling her what a farce his life had become. Despite his Christian upbringing, he no longer believed in God and didn't seem to even care that he had killed women and children. He did not send the letter; that would have been too shocking for innocent Thile to read. Instead he stuffed it at the bottom of his duffel bag inside his mother's Bible. Perhaps, he told himself, it would do some good in there.

The war continued on, and in February 1949 Andrew's company was ordered to move out in a major new push against the rebel enemy. Andrew knew that his pet gibbon could not travel with the company and would have to be let go. So a fellow soldier drove Andrew and the gibbon deep into the jungle. "You have to stay here," Andrew told his faithful little companion. Somehow the gibbon seemed to understand, because it stood perfectly still as Andrew got back in the jeep and sped off. Andrew looked behind, and there was the gibbon, standing and staring at him, making no attempt to follow. A deep sense of loneliness crept through Andrew. He would miss his pet. The gibbon had often seemed more human than ape.

Things were different once the gibbon was gone. Not only had he lost his companion, but also, after more than two years of combat, Andrew had lost his will to fight. He still wore his yellow straw hat and led the craziest raids, not caring whether he lived or died.

Three weeks after setting the gibbon free, Andrew was on patrol amid rice paddies outside of Jakarta. As his squad made their way along, wading in ankle-deep water and mud, the enemy opened fire on them. Suddenly bullets seemed to erupt from all around them.

"It's an ambush," Andrew heard one of his fellow soldiers bellow. "They've got us hemmed in on three sides."

Andrew fired off round after round from his rifle at the enemy. Then all of a sudden he felt a sting in his ankle. Pain surged up his leg, causing him to fall to his knees in the rice paddy. When he looked down to see what the problem was, Andrew saw blood oozing from a hole in his right combat boot. He looked closer and saw that an enemy bullet had gone right through his ankle.

"I'm hit," Andrew screamed.

Moments later two medics arrived and slid him onto a stretcher. Crouching low, they carried Andrew away, the yellow straw hat still on his head.

Somewhere along the way Andrew passed out from the searing pain in his right ankle. When he came to, he was in a field hospital. He could hear a nurse and doctor talking above him.

"I think we should try to save the leg first," he heard the doctor say.

"But his ankle is a real mess," the nurse responded.

"I know," the doctor replied, "and we may well yet have to amputate it."

The doctor shot local anesthetic from a syringe into Andrew's lower leg, and slowly the pain in Andrew's ankle began to subside as the doctor set to work on the injured ankle.

When his yellow straw hat fell off during the operation, Andrew asked the nurse to pick it up and put it back on his head. As she did so, he thought about how unlucky he had been. He had worn the hat so that someone would shoot him in the head and kill him. But instead he had been shot in the ankle, and at twenty years of age he would most likely spend the rest of his life crippled. In an instant, and without any fanfare, Andrew's war was over—but not his life.

Chapter 7

Home at Last

One day turned into another and then another as Andrew lay flat on his back in a Franciscan hospital in Jakarta. The plaster cast on his right leg stretched from his toes to his thigh, immobilizing him. The Catholic nuns who took care of him said that he should feel blessed because the doctor had been able to save his leg. But the word *blessed* was not in Andrew's vocabulary; *cursed* was a better choice of words for him.

Just as he had felt when his brother Bas was dying, Andrew now wished that he could die, but he seemed cursed to live the life of a cripple. Worse still, the war was winding down, and the Dutch were on the losing side. Indonesia, with the backing of the newly formed United Nations, was to become an independent nation. This was a bitter pill for Andrew to swallow. As he lay on his back in bed during the day, he thought about his grand adventure and what a nightmare it had turned into. And at night, when he could sleep, Andrew dreamed of the dead woman and her baby lying in a pool of blood.

A week after being injured, Andrew received his first visitor, Jan Zwart, a soldier from his company. The visit was supposed to have lifted Andrew's spirits, but it had the opposite effect. Jan explained how the Communists and PNI were using every tactical advantage in the fighting and that many soldiers from their company were being killed. In fact, Jan recounted, only eight soldiers were left of the original ninety men who had made up the company. But this was not what threw Andrew into deep despair. It was a letter he had written.

In the last few weeks before he was wounded, Andrew had taken up the habit of writing to Thile, telling her his deepest thoughts and describing the most vile things he had done that day. The list was sometimes long and disgusting. Even as he wrote the letters, Andrew knew that he would never send them. They were too horrible to show to anyone. Instead, he kept the letters in his duffel bag for a day or two, and then he would take them out and burn them. But one of these letters was still in his bag when he was shot in the ankle. And now he lay in agony in bed, listening to Jan cheerfully telling him that one of their friends had found the letter in his bag, looked up Thile's address in Andrew's address book, and mailed it off to her. Andrew was appalled. He could not imagine what Thile would do when she read all of the things he had written. He wanted to roll over and die.

"And I brought you this," Jan concluded. "It was in your things too." He pulled out Andrew's mother's Bible and laid it on the night table beside the bed.

"Thanks," Andrew muttered, sure that he would never open it.

Jan was one of the few visitors Andrew had in the hospital. Through the long days of recuperation, Andrew grew lonely and found himself thinking often of home. How was his sister Geltje? She had recently married, and Andrew tried to imagine the wedding without him or their mother present. Ben had written to say that he also was engaged but was postponing the wedding until Andrew got home.

The only ray of sunshine in Andrew's world was the Franciscan nuns who ran the hospital and nursed the patients. The nuns laughed and sang their way around the wards, even when they had to do the most disagreeable duties, such as swilling out the bedpans or changing soiled bandages. Andrew watched and waited to catch one of them in a bad mood, but he never did. One day he asked Sister Patrice, who was tending to him, why the nuns were so happy all the time.

"Andrew," Sister Patrice replied with a twinkle in her eye, "you are a good Dutch boy. Of course you know the answer. It's the love of Christ. Why, it's right here in the book beside your bed, isn't it?" She patted the Bible.

Andrew gulped. Sister Patrice sounded just like his mother used to sound.

Later that day Andrew was so bored that he decided to open the Bible and read it. He started reading at the very beginning, with God creating the heavens and the earth. It was the same story he had heard as a small boy in Sunday school, but now somehow it seemed different—alive, real. For the first time in his life, Andrew could not put the Bible down.

From then on, Andrew spent each day reading the Bible until he had made it all the way to the end of the New Testament. Some of the things that he read were mind-boggling, and he wondered whether some of the events had really happened and what it all meant to his life if they were true.

Such questions bothered Andrew, and even though he doubted that Thile would ever write to him again, he wrote to her, asking for answers to some of his questions. Much to his surprise, Thile wrote back telling Andrew that she had received his letter about the terrible things he had done and urging him to ask for and accept God's forgiveness for doing them. On one level Thile's letter made sense to Andrew, yet he could not bring himself to believe that if there was a God, He would be willing to forgive him for killing innocent women and children. It just did not seem possible.

Two months rolled by as Andrew studied the Bible and waited for his cast to come off. When it finally did, his right leg was shriveled and useless. The doctors tried to encourage Andrew by telling him that if he worked really hard on his exercises, one day he would be able to walk with a cane. But all Andrew could think of was running over the polder as a teenager. Now those days were gone, and at twenty years of age, he felt like an old man whose best days were behind him.

Andrew was fitted with a pair of crutches, and as soon as he could hobble around, he found the only comfort he knew—a bottle of gin at the nearest bar. For several weeks he stayed in the hospital during the day and went out drinking at night. Then, in May 1949, Andrew received word that the army was ready to ship him back to Holland. The idea of going home filled him with dread. What would people think of him, with his crippled leg and his cynical view of life? They had no idea what he had been through in Indonesia, and he did not know how to explain it to them.

On the afternoon before he was to be discharged from the hospital, Sister Patrice came to wish Andrew a happy twenty-first birthday and to tell him a story.

"Do you know how the natives catch monkeys out in the jungle?" Sister Patrice began.

"No. How?" Andrew replied.

"Well, a monkey won't let go of something he wants once he has grasped it, even if it means losing his freedom. The natives know this, and they exploit it. They take a coconut and make a small opening in it, just big enough for a monkey to slip his hand through, and then they drop a pebble into the coconut. They place the coconut by a bush and wait for a monkey to come along.

"When a monkey finally comes by, he is so curious that he picks up the coconut and shakes it. When he hears the pebble inside, he peers in and then slides his hand through the hole to grasp the pebble. When he tries to pull out his hand wrapped around the pebble, it will not fit back out through the hole. But the monkey will not let go of the pebble, even when the natives approach and capture him.

"Andrew, you are a little like that monkey. You are holding onto something—something that is keeping you from your freedom—and you will not let it go."

Andrew stared blankly at Sister Patrice. He had no idea what she thought he might be holding onto, and he didn't care. Instead, that night Andrew celebrated both his release from the hospital and his birthday the same way he celebrated most things, by drinking until he forgot who or where he was.

The voyage home to Holland was very different from the trip out to the Dutch East Indies three years before. Many of the men traveling on the ship were badly injured, and hardly anyone spoke during mealtimes. Andrew understood the silence. The men did not have much to talk about. He was sure that, like him, they were all thinking about how they had failed in their mission to keep Indonesia a Dutch colony. In fact, just four days before they set sail from Jakarta, the Dutch government had bowed to pressure from the United Nations and agreed to create a free Indonesia. As a result, General Spoor, the Dutch commander of Indonesia, had resigned his position.

Just as the ship docked in Rotterdam, the news was released that General Spoor had died of a heart attack. It seemed ironic to Andrew that on the same day that he was coming home as a "proud" soldier, the general's death was focusing the nation's attention on the humiliating defeat in Indonesia.

Upon his arrival in Rotterdam, Andrew was given leave to return home to his village before reporting to the rehabilitation unit the army had assigned him to for therapy on his wounded leg.

Back in Sint Pancras, everything was much as Andrew had left it, although a new row of elm trees was sprouting along the dike road. The first person Andrew saw was his sister Geltje. When Geltje spotted Andrew through the window, she rushed out across the little bridge to meet him. Soon Andrew was in the van der Bijl house, surrounded by his family and being introduced to his new brother-in-law Arie and to Ben's fiancée.

After everyone had welcomed him home, Andrew's other sister, Maartje, nudged his arm and asked, "Do you want to see Mama's grave?"

Andrew nodded. It was the one thing he wanted to do more than anything else, but his leg hurt so badly from walking from the bus stop to the house that he was afraid that he would not be able to make it to the cemetery.

"We can use Papa's bike, if you like," Maartje suggested.

Andrew nodded, stood up stiffly, and followed Maartje outside, leaning heavily on his cane. He wheeled the bike out onto the dike road. He threw his right leg over the bike so that it rested on the crossbar. Then Andrew hopped along on one leg, letting the bicycle carry the weight of his injured leg. It was not an elegant way to travel, and Andrew was glad that it was only five hundred yards to the village cemetery. He did not want to meet anyone along the way who would see him using the bike in this awkward manner.

At the cemetery the grass covering Andrew's mother's grave had not yet completely grown back, and a small vase holding fresh flowers sat on top of the grave. As Andrew stared down at the grave, he thought of the last time he had seen his mother. Was it possible that he had been that young man full of hope and bravado, imagining that war—any war—was some kind of grand adventure?

Andrew had so many things that he wanted to say to his mother, but he felt uncomfortable saying them in front of Maartje. He promised himself that he would soon return alone to the gravesite. That night, when Andrew had answered all the easy questions about living in Indonesia and Cornelius had pumped him about the habits of the gibbon,

Andrew set out by himself for the cemetery. When he got there, he sat down and wept.

"I did things I will never forgive myself for—things you would not think your boy was capable of," Andrew said. "Mama, help me. I need to find my way back, but I don't think I can. What am I going to do with the rest of my life?"

Somewhere in the back of his mind Andrew had hoped that this moment sitting beside his mother's grave would bring him peace and answers. But he soon discovered that there were none. An hour and a half later, he wiped the tears from his eyes and half rode, half walked home again.

The following day Andrew ate breakfast with his family and then decided to brave the village. Leaning heavily on his cane (he did not want to be seen on his crutches), Andrew hobbled down the dike road. The people he met along the way had known him his entire life, yet as they greeted him, they were polite but distant. They made small talk and asked him *where* he had hurt his leg, but not *how*. No one mentioned the latest news that the remaining Dutch troops were preparing to be evacuated from Indonesia.

Andrew was embarrassed talking with his family and with the people he met in the village about his experiences, but he longed for someone to have a serious conversation with. Somehow he found himself walking toward the Whetstra home. Mr. and Mrs. Whetstra greeted Andrew like a long-lost son. Mrs. Whetstra bustled around making coffee and buttering buns, while Mr. Whetstra peppered Andrew with questions.

Andrew was relieved to find someone who was genuinely interested both in what he had been through and in the fall of Indonesia. After several minutes, Mr. Whetstra paused and then asked, "So Andrew, was it the great adventure you were looking for?"

"No," Andrew replied, embarrassed as he thought back to his earlier excitement about joining the army.

"Well then," Mr. Whetstra said, patting him on the back, "we will just have to keep praying for you, won't we?"

Andrew looked down at his crippled right leg and laughed bitterly. "There are no more adventures left in my future," he said.

The conversation went dead after this, and Andrew regretted his outburst. Deep down he longed to talk to someone about his life, or the shell of it that was left, but he could not bring himself to be honest about his fears for the future. Instead he muttered some excuse and left the Whetstras' house.

"Come back and see us soon," Mr. Whetstra said as Andrew left, but Andrew did not know whether he would. The Whetstras were just too nice for a young man who had done the things he had done.

As he hobbled along, leaning more heavily than ever on his cane, Andrew wondered whom he could visit next. Kees, his friend from the Resistance, popped into his mind. Andrew remembered Kees as a wild, daring boy. Surely, Andrew reasoned, if anyone wanted to hear tales of commando raids and ambushes in Indonesia, it would be Kees. When Andrew arrived at the house, Kees's mother directed him upstairs to Kees's bedroom.

Andrew half walked, half pulled himself up the stairs. He found Kees bent over a book, studying hard. Kees greeted Andrew warmly and cleared a space on the bed for him to sit down. After a few awkward moments, Andrew asked Kees what he was studying.

"I've found what I want to do with my life," Kees said, holding up a Bible study book.

Andrew felt a fake smile freeze on his face. "What?" he asked, although he had already guessed the answer.

"I'm going to become a minister," Kees announced enthusiastically.

There was a longer silence as Andrew tried to think of something to say. He wanted to scream, *"But Kees, you were a daredevil, my boyhood hero. Don't throw your life away on religion!"* Instead he made an excuse about leaving and dragged himself down the stairs and out the door, mumbling farewell to Kees's mother as he left.

Back on the dike road, Andrew felt an overwhelming pressure in his chest. Nothing was turning out the way he had thought it would. Most people were being polite, though they were not particularly interested in his experiences, and the only ones who were interested wanted to talk to him about God. Andrew had spent three years in Indonesia, longing to be home, and now home was the last place on earth he wanted to be.

Chapter 8

Letting Go of Himself

Andrew was relieved to say good-bye to Sint Pancras. The army had arranged for him to enter a rehabilitation program at a veterans' hospital in Doorn, about sixty miles away. At the hospital Andrew found it strangely comforting to be around other young men who had suffered similar experiences to his. No one stared at his cane, and if someone wanted to know how he had injured his leg, the person would ask Andrew directly and listen without grimacing through the explanation.

The best thing of all about Doorn for Andrew was that it was situated not too far from Gorkum and Thile's home. On his first weekend of leave, Andrew made a beeline for Thile's house. But things did not start out well. The bus was so crowded that it had standing room only, and a woman stood up to allow Andrew to take her seat. Although he knew he could not stand the entire way, Andrew was humiliated to think that he looked so disabled.

When Andrew finally got to Thile's house, things got worse. Although he had often imagined the wonderful moment of meeting Thile again, in reality their meeting was tense. Thile wanted to know how Andrew was doing with his Bible reading, and Andrew had to admit that he had not picked the Bible up since arriving home. Thile looked very disappointed. "Andrew, God is waiting to turn your life around and shape you into something new. Why don't you let Him?" she asked.

It was the kind of question Mr. Whetstra might have asked, but Andrew was in no mood to reflect on his spiritual condition. Although he wanted to retaliate to the question with some wisecrack, instead he became sullen. Everyone, it seemed, had some idea or plan for how to "make him better." Yet despite the unexpected turns in their conversation, Andrew enjoyed his visit with Thile and promised that he would return to see her again when he next got leave. It was several weeks, however, before Andrew got more leave, so he contented himself with writing to Thile.

About a month after his visit with Thile, Andrew had an experience that he could not put into words. It all started when a pretty, blonde young woman came into his ward at the veterans' hospital. The woman invited Andrew and the other twenty men he shared the ward with to attend a revival meeting that evening. She announced that a bus had been arranged to transport those who wanted to go to the meeting site. The young men let out wolf whistles at her as she left the ward and promised that they would come to the meeting. Surprisingly, by six thirty in the evening, all of the men from the ward were dressed in their best clothes and were waiting in line at the hospital door for the bus to arrive.

Andrew and his friend Pier, who shared the bed next to him in the ward, hung at the back of the line. Earlier in the afternoon Pier had sneaked into town and bought a bottle of gin, and now he and Andrew stood in line, taking large swigs from the bottle. By the time the bus arrived at seven to pick the men up, Andrew was feeling the warm, comforting buzz of the alcohol enveloping him.

Andrew and Pier continued swigging the gin throughout the bus ride that took them to the outskirts of town, where a large tent had been erected for the meeting. Inside the tent Andrew and Pier found a seat at the back and drained the bottle of gin while they waited for the service to begin.

The service began when a man with deep-set eyes and a narrow face took the podium. To Andrew the man's face looked like that of a rat, and Andrew began to laugh out loud. Pier joined in the laughter, and the two men were still guffawing when the opening hymn ended. Andrew had no idea how disruptive his and Pier's behavior was until the rat-faced man announced, "Brothers and sisters, we have two men here tonight who are chained by the powers of a dark world." The man then began to pray out loud for Andrew and Pier.

As the man prayed, Andrew tried to control his laughter until his sides hurt. Finally he lost the battle and was soon guffawing louder than ever, so loud, in fact, that he drowned out the rat-faced man's prayer. Andrew watched in drunken delight as the obviously frustrated man gave up his prayer and told the choir to sing. The choir stood to its feet and began singing the song "Let My People Go."

When the choir reached the chorus to the song, everyone in the tent joined in the singing. By now Andrew and Pier were laughing uncontrollably. In fact, Andrew could not recall a time when he had laughed so much. It felt good to laugh, even if the laughter was alcohol induced.

The choir sang on through the second verse of the song, but when the audience again joined in for the chorus, Andrew noticed a curious thing. As they belted out "Let my people go," the words suddenly had a sobering effect on him. Andrew stopped laughing and listened to the words being sung around him. But instead of hearing "Let my people go," Andrew seemed to be hearing "Let me go," as though it were Andrew addressing some force outside of himself.

Andrew sat silently on the bus ride back to the hospital, contemplating the words of the song. What could they mean? And why had they seemed to speak to him?

The following morning Andrew awoke with a hangover. But he also awoke with something else—a deep desire to read his mother's Bible. All that day he carried the Bible with him, reading it whenever he had a spare moment. And much to his surprise, he wanted to read more the following day, and the day after that. Soon he had set himself a schedule to help guide him systematically through the whole Bible.

As a result of his Bible reading, Andrew had a much more enjoyable visit with Thile the next time he went to see her. He now wanted to discuss with Thile what he was reading in the Bible, and he enjoyed Thile's comments and observations. He enjoyed his conversations with Thile so much, in fact, that he decided he would ask her to marry him as soon as he was released from the army and had a steady job.

Andrew's release from the army and the rehabilitation center came in November 1949. The Dutch government gave Andrew a small severance allotment along with his discharge papers. Andrew used the money to buy a bicycle. The weeks of rehabilitation therapy had improved the strength in his right leg, but he still had a long way to go if he was to walk without a limp. Andrew decided that riding the bike around would both help to strengthen his leg and get him out onto the polders on which he had loved so much to run.

Since Andrew had nowhere else to go after his release from the hospital and the army, he went back home to Sint Pancras and moved in with his father. Although Andrew did not have a job, he did have a way to fill his days—he went to church, one service every night and two on Sundays. Some of the services were at the Reformed church in Sint Pancras, while others, such as the Salvation Army service in Alkmaar and the Baptist prayer meeting in Amsterdam, were a long bike ride away. Andrew did not care what denomination people belonged to as long as they believed the Bible and wanted to have fellowship with him. At the services he attended, Andrew took careful notes during the sermons and reviewed them the following day, rereading all the Bible passages mentioned and reflecting on their meaning and the meaning of the sermon to his life.

The van der Bijls were staunch members of the Dutch Reformed Church, and Andrew's church-attending actions did not please them. At first Andrew was oblivious to their concerns, until one day when his sister Maartje brought him a cup of tea. Andrew was sprawled out on his bed reading a psalm.

"Andrew," Maartje said shyly, "I know you have been through a lot, and I don't want to hurt your feelings, but I am worried about the amount of time you spend in your bedroom. It's not normal. And all this riding around to churches. You never used to go to service even once on Sunday, and now you go every day. Don't you think it's a bit much?"

Andrew stared at his sister. "I just feel like I have to, Maartje. I wish I knew what was happening to me."

Maartje sighed. "Well, we are worried, and Papa especially..." Her voice trailed off. "Papa says it's shell shock."

Andrew did not know what to say next, and Maartje put down the cup of tea and quietly left the room.

As he thought back on his behavior since arriving home from the rehabilitation unit, Andrew had to admit that it probably did look strange to people. *But am I in danger of becoming one of those religious kooks ranting on the streets in Amsterdam? Or even becoming like the Whetstras, quoting Bible verses for every situation. Is that what I'm turning into?* These were sobering questions, and Andrew's tea grew cold as he pondered them. In the end he could not come up with an answer. All he knew was that he felt powerless to resist the fellowship of Christians wherever he could find it. He decided to discuss his family's concerns with Thile. Surely she would know what to do. But Thile proved to be anything but comforting.

"I have been wondering that too, Andy!" Thile confided. "I just didn't know how to bring up the subject."

"What do you mean?" Andrew asked, thinking that if Thile thought like the members of his family, he must look more weird than he had ever imagined.

"Well," she continued awkwardly, "I know you have to have something to hold onto now that you are back from the army, but do you have to be so… so fanatical about it? You don't want to burn yourself out. Why don't you read other books sometimes or go to the movies with me?"

Despite Thile's suggestion, Andrew found that

he could not be bothered doing other things. He loved to read the Bible, pray, and go to church. Nothing else was remotely interesting to him. Then one night, soon after New Year 1950, Andrew had an experience that convinced him he was on track.

It was a cold, blustery night. The wind howled around the van der Bijl house, and sleet blew horizontally across the polder. Andrew lay in bed with the blankets pulled up tightly beneath his chin to keep warm. As he stared at the darkened ceiling, the story that Sister Patrice had told him before he left Indonesia—and especially her words about how a monkey won't let go of something—flooded his memory. He also thought about the words of the song from the revival meeting in Doorn: "Let my people go." *What am I holding onto?* Andrew asked himself. Then the answer suddenly came to him—he had to let go of himself. He had to place his life fully and completely in God's hands. Quietly, in barely more than a whisper, Andrew opened his mouth and prayed. "Lord, if You will show me the way, I will follow You. Amen."

This simple prayer led to instant changes in Andrew's life. For the first time in years, Andrew felt clean inside, as if his mind had been scrubbed out. He could not wait to tell someone about his experience, and the only people he was sure would understand what had happened to him were the Whetstras and Kees. Andrew went and told Mr. and Mrs. Whetstra about his experience, and they were both delighted for him. Kees also was delighted with the news, and he asked Andrew to become his prayer and Bible study partner.

In the spring of 1950, just as the tulips were beginning to break through the soggy ground, Andrew and Kees decided to go to Amsterdam together to hear a well-known Dutch evangelist named Arne Donker. Andrew was surprised at how much he enjoyed Pastor Donker's message, especially since he was feeling a little out of place among such an exuberant crowd. He began to feel truly uncomfortable, however, when Pastor Donker announced, "I have the feeling something unique is taking place here tonight. Someone in this audience is going to give himself as a missionary."

Andrew sneaked a look at Kees, and both men rolled their eyes at the same time. Andrew knew that they were both thinking the same thing: *Let's get out of here before this turns weird.* Without saying a word, they stood up and sidestepped their way to the end of the row. But so many people turned to look at them expectantly as they did so that they both sat down in the empty seats at the end of the row.

"Better wait until this is over," Kees whispered to Andrew.

No one else in the auditorium had moved, but Arne Donker did not back down. "There is a life of constant danger and risk waiting to be claimed tonight—by a young man, I think."

Andrew looked straight ahead. Then, without

thinking about what he was doing, he got back to his feet. Kees also stood up, and like two lemmings returning to the sea, Andrew and Kees marched single file toward the front of the auditorium.

Andrew heard Pastor Donker say, "There you are, not one but two of you! Wonderful. Come all the way to the front."

The aisle seemed to stretch on forever, but Andrew and Kees did not stop until they had reached the front of the auditorium.

"Kneel down, boys. I want to pray for you," Pastor Donker said.

Andrew and Kees knelt obediently, and Pastor Donker began to pray. Though Andrew did not take in any of what the pastor was praying, he did hear the instructions the pastor gave after finishing praying. "Make sure I talk to you two before you leave tonight."

The whole incident seemed surreal to Andrew as he sat in the front row while the congregation sang the closing hymn. When the meeting was over and everyone got up to leave, Andrew wanted to get up too and melt into the crowd. He felt compelled, however, to stay put and wait for the pastor to disentangle himself from the group of people who had gathered around him and were peppering him with questions.

Finally, when the hall was nearly empty, Pastor Donker strode over to the front-row pew. "So what are your names?" he asked.

"Andrew and Kees," Andrew quickly replied, hoping to avoid using last names or mentioning any other details, such as where they came from.

"Great. Andrew and Kees. Fine names. Are you two ready for your first assignment?"

Andrew felt sick in the pit of his stomach. He did not know why he had walked up to the front, but he was one hundred percent sure that it had not been to sign on as Pastor Donker's puppet!

"Where are you from?" the pastor asked.

"Sint Pancras," Andrew muttered.

"Both of you?"

Kees nodded.

"Good, good. It is biblical to work in pairs. The New Testament model is for missionaries to begin in their own towns, their own backyards, and preach the gospel and then move out from there."

Andrew smiled weakly, afraid of what he was going to hear next.

"So here's what you are going to do. Both of you are to prepare a short testimony, and I will come to Sint Pancras next Saturday. At one o'clock we will hold an open-air meeting outside the mayor's house. I'll be there to support you and offer a few closing thoughts."

Andrew felt the blood draining from his face. If his family thought he was turning into a religious fanatic before, what would they think when he started preaching in the street—and not just any street, but the main street in Sint Pancras!

More than anything else, Andrew wanted to say no. *No,* he would not make a fool of himself. *No,* he would not prepare a testimony. *No,* he had not even intended to come down to the front. But try as he might, the word would not come out of his mouth. Instead Andrew found himself nodding approvingly and giving Arne Donker his address.

Andrew and Kees walked out of the auditorium in stunned silence. Andrew wished that Kees had spoken up, and he was sure that Kees wished the same thing of him. But neither of them had spoken up, and now they were stuck. *There is one thing for sure,* Andrew told himself as they made their way home. *I am going to keep this as quiet as possible. I'm not going to invite a single person to attend the meeting, and if we're lucky, maybe no one will notice us.*

Chapter 9

Headed for an Unknown Adventure

As one o'clock on Saturday approached, Andrew made his way to the square in front of the mayor's house. Fear gripped him when he saw the crowd.

"We heard that you and Kees were going to speak. We have never had anyone in the village do anything like this before," a neighbor told Andrew as he pushed through the crowd.

Arne Donker had set up a small platform, and he and Kees were standing at the back of it. Pastor Donker shook Andrew's hand and then, after saying a prayer, climbed up onto the platform, where he welcomed the crowd and introduced Kees and Andrew. He then invited Kees to step forward and speak. Andrew listened from behind the platform, but he could not concentrate on a word Kees said. Beads of cold sweat formed on his brow. In all the dangerous battles he had been through in Indonesia, he had never felt this scared. His knees were even knocking.

Finally Kees finished speaking, and Pastor Donker invited Andrew to come forward and speak. The dreaded moment had arrived, and Andrew limped forward to the edge of the platform. He looked out on the crowd, and stern faces stared back at him. Andrew's mouth suddenly went dry, and his tongue felt furry as he began to speak. Andrew started to recite the testimony he had written out and memorized during the week, but the words seemed flat and dead to him, as if they were not reaching the ears of those in the crowd. He decided to abandon the prepared testimony and just speak from his heart.

"I did some terrible things when I was in the East Indies," he began, "things that I am not proud of. When I arrived home, I was lost. I felt dirty inside and guilty over the things I had done. It was as if chains were bound around me."

As Andrew spoke from his heart, he felt the fear drain away. And he noticed that the stern looks on the faces staring up at him began to dissolve. Some people even smiled, at him and others nodded their heads in agreement.

"I searched for freedom, for something to change the way I felt on the inside. And then one stormy night in January I found the freedom I was looking for. I found it when I laid my burden of guilt and shame at the feet of Jesus and surrendered myself to Him."

Following the open-air meeting, a few people in the village gave Andrew strange looks, but he did not care. He realized that they had probably expected him to do something "foolish" like that, anyway. But much to his surprise, when he looked back on the experience, Andrew had to admit to himself that he had enjoyed sharing his faith with others, so much so that he began to look for a way to become a missionary.

Once Thile understood that Andrew was serious about becoming a missionary, she pitched in and helped him to write letters inquiring about how to become a missionary with the Dutch Reformed Church. The replies he received to his letters all pointed in the same direction. Andrew needed to go to seminary and become an ordained minister. Once he was an ordained minister, he should work in a church for a few years and then seek a missionary position. But because Andrew had not attended high school, becoming an ordained minister would involve twelve years of study.

This was all too much for Andrew. He counted up the years. It would be 1962, and he would be at least thirty-four years old before he became an ordained minister. There was no way he could wait that long to follow his calling. Yet when Andrew explained this to people, they asked him where and what he was called to do. But he could not answer their questions. Although he felt a general call to follow God and do something, he was not sure what that was or where it would be. The idea of becoming a missionary seemed to come to a halt, and Andrew decided to get a job while he prayed some more about the whole issue.

The chocolate factory in Alkmaar, where Geltje's husband, Arie, worked, was hiring workers, and Andrew applied for a job there. He was hired as a delivery boy, pushing carts filled with chocolates from the assembly room to the shipping platform. The chocolate factory turned out to be a mission field of its own, and soon Andrew was helping to organize prayer meetings among the workers and taking many of his workmates with him to the weekend evangelistic rallies. To keep his missionary vision alive, he also bought theology books and studied them and began taking English lessons with Miss Meekle, a schoolteacher in the village.

On the weekends Andrew also visited Thile, who encouraged him, praising him for all the good changes that he was helping to bring at the factory. But though he had played a part in changing the atmosphere at the chocolate factory and had seen the conversion of several hardened young women there, Andrew knew that something was not right. Yes, the chocolate factory was a mission field, but it was not his mission field. Somewhere out there was a place where he belonged, and after two years of working at the factory, he became desperate to find that place.

The idea of becoming a missionary with the Dutch Reformed Church seemed more elusive than ever, and Andrew decided to see whether other mission agencies might accept him as a missionary. He could not think of why he had not done this before, except for the fact that Thile had been opposed to his going outside their Reformed Church circle.

As it turned out, Andrew was invited to hear a missionary from the Worldwide Evangelization Crusade (WEC) speak. He went expecting to hear about missionary opportunities around the world, and he was not disappointed. However, the speaker, an Englishman named Mr. Johnson, also explained that WEC missionaries lived by faith. By this Mr. Johnson meant that missionaries with the organization did not receive an income from any church or other organization but rather prayed and asked God to supply their needs.

Andrew had been interested in all that Mr. Johnson had to say up until he heard this piece of information. Suddenly he found his mind drifting off to think about all of the people he knew who lived by faith. These people were uncomfortable to be around and made him feel guilty if he spent any money or wore a nice jacket. But they also specialized in "hinting" about their physical needs. *So much for trusting God,* Andrew thought as the meeting came to a close.

The following evening, Andrew went for a bike ride with Kees. As they peddled along together, Kees peppered Andrew with questions about WEC.

Andrew did not have many answers for him, confessing that he had stopped paying attention when he learned that WEC missionaries lived by faith. However, he did have the address of the organization's training school in Glasgow, Scotland, and he suggested that since Kees was so interested in WEC, he might want to write there himself.

That is just what Kees did. Much to Andrew's surprise, Kees applied to and was accepted by WEC to train as a missionary. It all happened so quickly, and soon Kees was on his way to Scotland to train.

Kees wrote home to Andrew each week, describing the courses he was taking, the practical training he was getting, and the wonderful Christian fellowship he was enjoying. Soon Andrew was convinced that he should go too. He sent off an application to WEC. The response he received back was swift and encouraging. Yes, WEC would accept Andrew for the May 1953 intake. The date was only a few weeks away, and Andrew quickly gave notice at work that he was leaving and sold his books and his bicycle.

Andrew made a hurried visit to Gorkum to tell Thile the news in person. Thile was not pleased. To her anything that was not sanctioned by the Dutch Reformed Church was a waste of time, and she did not mince her words as she told Andrew so. But Andrew was too excited to be unduly upset by her response. He knew that Thile took a little while to get used to new plans, and he was sure that in the end she would see things his way.

April 20 was the day that Andrew was to set sail from Rotterdam for London. It was only a week away, and during that week three unexpected things happened to Andrew—all of them unpleasant!

The first unpleasant thing came in the form of a letter from Thile. In the letter Thile explained that her minister had told her that the Reformed Church would not recognize Andrew's training at WEC, and since Andrew did not seem to care about this fact, she did not want to see or hear from him again.

Andrew felt as though he had been slapped in the face—hard. He thought of the happy times he had enjoyed attending church with Thile and how beautiful she always looked when she said good-bye at the end of his visits. She was the most wonderful person he knew, and now she was ending their relationship. Although nothing formal had been said, Andrew had assumed that one day she would be his wife. But now it seemed that this was not going to be.

Before Andrew had time to properly process Thile's letter, which was a bitter blow, Miss Meekle came trotting along the dike road and over the foot-bridge into the van der Bijl yard. She knocked at the door, and Andrew opened it. Miss Meekle then immediately launched into a confession.

"Andrew," she began, "I think you need to know that I have never actually heard English being spoken. But I know that my grammar is right, because I correspond with a woman in England, and she says I write perfectly..." Her voice trailed off. "But as far as the pronunciation goes, well...I can't be sure if I am teaching it right." With that she turned and hurried off.

Andrew could barely take in her revelation. He had labored hard learning to speak and understand English so that he would be able to understand the lectures in Scotland and talk to people there. Now he was left wondering whether the other missionary trainees would understand a word he said in English.

Three days later, more devastating news arrived, and it too came in the form of a letter. The letter, which was from WEC, contained an apology for any inconvenience to Andrew along with an explanation that there was no room for him in the program at the moment and he should reapply in two years.

Two years! Andrew had already quit his job, sold his bicycle, told his family he was leaving, and used all of his savings to buy a one-way ticket to London. And now WEC was asking him to delay his coming for two years! It was almost more than Andrew could bear, and he struggled to find some meaning in all that had happened to him that week. Did God want him to stay at home, get another job, and marry Thile? Or did He want Andrew to find someone who had actually heard English spoken and take lessons from that person? These were two possibilities, but as Andrew prayed about the situation, a peace descended over him, and one word came into his mind: *Go.*

Although it did not make much sense, since there was no position waiting for him at the other end, Andrew decided to follow the leading and go. He did not tell his family that WEC could not take him at the present time. Instead he carried on with his packing and saying good-bye to friends and family in the village. Two days later Andrew was on a bus bound for Rotterdam, where he would board the ship for the trip to London and whatever adventure lay beyond.

Chapter 10

An Experiment in Trusting God

Andrew stood in the street outside the train station in London, the address of the WEC headquarters in his hand. When he spotted a policeman in a tall, black hat, he walked over to him. "Can you tell me how to get here?" he asked, holding up the piece of paper.

The policeman looked puzzled for a moment and then pointed westward. He rattled off a string of instructions, but Andrew could not understand a single word, and he wondered whether the policeman was actually speaking English. Still, he had a direction in which to head, so he picked up his suitcase and began walking west. Double-decker buses whizzed by, and taxicabs honked their horns, but Andrew hoped to be able to walk to WEC headquarters. He had little money left, and he did not want to waste it on public transportation.

After walking for about half a mile, Andrew asked another person for directions. He got the same unintelligible answer he had from the policeman, only this time the person pointed east. Andrew sighed. He had been in London less than an hour, and he already knew two things: Miss Meekle's "English" was not understood in England, and he would have to take a taxi to reach his destination.

Andrew hailed a taxicab, and ten minutes later the cab pulled up in front of a shabby, two-story building. Andrew paid the driver and got out. Sure enough, a sign above the door read "Worldwide Evangelization Crusade."

Much to Andrew's surprise, a man who spoke some Dutch welcomed him at the door.

"My name is Andrew van der Bijl," he said. "I just got here from Holland."

The man frowned. "Andrew van der Bijl? Didn't you get the letter explaining that we don't have a place for you at present?"

"Yes, I got it," Andrew replied, "but I decided to come anyway so that I would be ready when a place opens up for me."

The man smiled. "All right then. You are here now, so welcome. Come on in, and I'll show you a bed. We can't have you stay here indefinitely, but you can stay a few days until we sort something out."

Relief flooded through Andrew. Until this point he had not realized just how much he needed to hear someone say "welcome" and offer to help work things out.

As it turned out, Andrew stayed at WEC headquarters for nearly two months. He was put to work painting the shabby outside of the building. The job was simple enough, unlike learning "English" English, which proved to be a much more stressful task. Andrew was grateful that he had not gone straight to the training school in Glasgow, as he would not have understood anything that was said, nor would he have been able to make himself understood. As hard as it was living at WEC headquarters and practicing English, he realized it would have been a hundred times more difficult trying to master the language as a student.

To help himself, Andrew read through a King James Bible that someone gave him. He kept an English dictionary nearby to look up any words that he did not know. But it was not the written word that gave him the most trouble; it was the spoken word. The Dutch language has no *th* sound, and Andrew found this sound difficult to pronounce. When he was asked to give a devotional talk one morning, he chose the text "Receive thy sight, thy faith hath saved thee." But the best pronunciation he could manage was, "Receive die side, die fade had saved dee." He felt very foolish for having chosen a verse with so many *th*'s in it.

By mid-June the painting job was complete, and someone else needed Andrew's bed. Andrew went to Kent, south of London, to stay with Mr. and Mrs. Hopkins. Mr. Hopkins was a building contractor and a generous donor to WEC. Andrew was not surprised to discover that Mr. and Mrs. Hopkins lived in a simple, cozy house, because he had been told that they gave away ninety percent of their income to missionary societies.

Before long, Uncle Hoppy and Mother Hoppy, as everyone called Mr. and Mrs. Hopkins, became like a second set of parents to Andrew. Mother Hoppy was an invalid, much like Andrew's mother had been, and she had the same faith and determination to live each day for God. Andrew would often come home at night to find a drunk or a prostitute whom Mother Hoppy was witnessing to staying in the house. In the morning the person would be fed a good breakfast, given a coat if he or she needed one, and prayed for before he or she left.

Andrew felt so at home with the Hopkins family that when he received word that he could begin his WEC training sooner than expected, he was sorry to be leaving them. In September 1953 Andrew thanked the Hopkinses for the wonderful care and friendship they had given him and caught the train to Glasgow.

After arriving in Glasgow, Andrew found his way to Number 10 Prince Albert Road, where the WEC training school was located. The building that housed the school was a large, two-story house set on a corner. It was surrounded by a stone wall, and on the archway over the gate were painted the words *Have Faith In God*. Andrew walked under the archway and up to the front door. He knocked, and moments later the door swung open. Much to Andrew's delight, there stood Kees. The two of them embraced and greeted each other, and then Kees showed Andrew upstairs to his room and introduced him to his three roommates.

After Andrew had settled in, Kees took him to meet the director of the training school, Stewart Dinnen. Andrew shook Stewart's hand, and then Stewart told him a little about the philosophy of the school.

"Andrew," he began, "the purpose of this training school is to teach our students that they can trust God to do what He has said He would do. You don't go from here into traditional mission fields. You go into new territory. Graduates of the school are on their own. They can't be effective if they're afraid or if they doubt that God really means what He says in His Word. I hope that's the kind of training you are looking for in coming here, Andrew."

"Yes, sir. That is exactly the kind of training I am looking for," Andrew replied.

After Andrew had settled into the school, he was once again glad that he had not come directly to Glasgow from Holland. Even though his English was much better after his time in London, he had a great deal of trouble understanding the Glaswegian accent. However, he persevered because one of his class assignments was to practice one-on-one evangelism in the streets.

Andrew went to share the gospel in one of the worst areas in Glasgow—a slum called Patrick, which had such a reputation for violence that even policemen would not walk its streets alone. But because Andrew believed that this was where God wanted him to go, off he went to Patrick. He could scarcely believe the condition of the place the first time he saw it. Everything was dark and dank. The bulbs in the streetlights were broken or had been stolen, and rotting garbage was piled everywhere in the streets. Children with runny noses and draped in threadbare rags eyed him suspiciously as he made his way along the street, carrying a pile of gospel tracts. Andrew had never encountered a place like this in Holland. The Dutch penchant for order and cleanliness would never allow such a place to exist.

On the corner of each block were smoke-filled pubs where glassy-eyed men sat getting drunk, usually spending their family's food money on cheap whiskey. Andrew went into the pubs and asked the proprietors if he could hand out tracts in their establishment. None of them refused, and Andrew went about giving away tracts to the pub patrons and talking to anyone he could strike up a conversation with.

At one pub Andrew met a man named Jack Kearney. Jack was totally drunk, but he took one of the tracts and asked Andrew to visit him at his house the following evening. Andrew agreed to do that, and the next evening he and Albert, one of his friends from the training school, made their way up four flights of stairs to Jack's apartment. As with the streetlights outside, the lightbulbs that lit the stairway had been either broken or stolen. Andrew and Albert were forced to pick their way up the stairs in total darkness, trying their best to avoid the broken beer bottles on the steps.

The two men located the door to the apartment and knocked. Jack opened the door, and Andrew could clearly see that he was still drunk. Jack's eyes were glazed, he wobbled on his feet, and his breath stank of stale whiskey. "Come in," Jack said, motioning Andrew and Albert in.

Inside the apartment was dingy, lit by a single lightbulb. The wallpaper was stained brown and peeling off the walls, and the paint was peeling from the ceiling. Moldering bread crusts and scraps of food were spread about the kitchen counter and table, and the sink was piled high with dirty dishes.

"Let me fix you a cup of tea," Jack said, and with that he turned and pulled three dirty cups from the sink. He did not bother to wash them; he just rubbed them with a stained dish towel.

Andrew and Albert looked at each other, their eyes wide, but they did not say a word. Andrew knew that it would be insulting to turn down Jack's offer of a cup of tea, even if the cups were not clean.

Several minutes later Jack laid three cups full of tea on the table. As they sipped the tea, the three men talked, with Jack asking Andrew question after question about his life in Holland and his experiences in Indonesia.

"So, Dutchman, since you were in the army, tell me, what's the first law of war?" Jack finally asked.

Andrew thought for a moment and then lifted his eyes to stare into Jack's stubbled face. "It's your life or mine. That's the law of war, Jack," he said.

"Right, you're exactly right," Jack said. With that he pushed himself up from the table, walked to the sideboard behind Andrew, opened a drawer, and pulled something out. It was a cutthroat razor. Jack flicked the razor open, spun around, and held the razor to Andrew's throat. "And I'm going to kill you," he said.

Albert sat across the table from Andrew, who could see that his friend was too petrified to do anything but pray. Meanwhile Andrew thought fast. He had no doubt that Jack, in his drunken condition, was well capable of slitting his throat with the razor.

"You're right, Jack. It is my life or yours, but because of that you can't do this. Someone has already died to save your life and mine. His name is Jesus Christ."

Andrew felt Jack press the razor harder to his neck. He felt the sharp blade nicking the skin at his throat. "Jack, Jesus came into the world because of these laws of war and because of the spiritual warfare where only one man can win and the other lose," Andrew continued. "One has to die so that the other will live. And that's what Jesus Christ did. He died so that you might live, Jack."

Jack held completely still for a moment. Andrew's heart thumped in his chest as he waited to see what Jack would do. Would he let him go or slit his throat? Much to his relief, Andrew felt Jack release the pressure on the razor and move it away from his throat. Jack stepped back, closed the razor, and dropped it in the drawer.

Thinking quickly, Andrew said, "Thank you for putting the razor away, Jack. We'll be on our way now, but I'll come back and talk some more with you about Jesus."

Jack nodded silently as Andrew and Albert headed out of the apartment and down the darkened stairs as fast as they could. They were both ashen-faced and shaking by the time they made it out into the street.

The follow evening Andrew went back to see Jack, though this time he decided not to take Albert with him. In fear and trepidation Andrew made his way back up the stairs to Jack's apartment. He knocked gingerly on the door. Jack opened it, and much to Andrew's relief, although he looked terrible, with big, black rings under his eyes, Jack was not drunk.

"I'm sorry about last night," Jack apologized. "It was a terrible thing to do to you. It's the alcohol. It makes me do terrible things."

"That's okay, Jack. I understand," Andrew said as he stepped inside Jack's apartment. "You know, Jesus still loves you, Jack. He really does. Why don't you pray and ask Him to come into your life and change it," Andrew continued.

Much to Andrew's surprise, Jack sank to his knees in the kitchen and began pouring his heart out to God, asking Him to forgive him and change his life. "I'm a really bad person, Jesus, but I really do want to follow You. Please forgive me and accept me," Jack prayed.

That night, when Andrew left Jack's apartment, he almost floated down the darkened stairs. Jack Kearney, the hard-drinking Scotsman from the slums who had wanted to slit Andrew's throat, had become a Christian.

Andrew visited Jack several more times, and each time he left the apartment, he was amazed at the changes taking place in Jack. God had really touched and changed Jack's life.

The first term of the training school passed quickly. Since there were no paid workers at WEC, all of the students had to pitch in and help with the chores. Andrew took his turn doing laundry, cooking meals, and scrubbing the toilets.

The school offered other practical lessons as well. Everyone learned how to make a shelter out of fern fronds, how to strip and rebuild a car engine, and how to form clay into a drinking vessel. These were important skills because many of the WEC graduates were headed out to live in primitive conditions in far-off lands. For his part, Andrew had no idea where God might call him, but he did not let it worry him. For now he had more than enough to concentrate on.

During his first term in the school, one of the writers Andrew came to enjoy reading was a Scottish evangelist named Oswald Chambers. Chambers had died in 1917, but his devotional book *My Utmost for His Highest* inspired Andrew, especially so when

Andrew suffered a back problem and had to lie in bed for days at a time. During this time Andrew decided to write a letter to Oswald Chambers's widow, an elderly woman named Bibby.

Just before Christmas Andrew received a gracious reply from Bibby Chambers. In her letter Bibby invited Andrew to visit her sometime. Andrew wrote straight back, suggesting that he come for Christmas.

When he told his classmates what he had done, they were aghast. "You can't just invite yourself to stay with someone that famous," they told him. But Andrew did not understand their reasoning. Bibby Chambers had invited him to visit, and he would love to go.

So at Christmas Andrew set out by train for southern England and spent the holiday season at the Chambers home. He found Bibby to be a wonderful hostess. She even let him read some of her late husband's original texts. As a result of the stay, Andrew and Bibby Chambers became good friends.

After his visit to southern England, it was back to Scotland for another term at the training school. This time something special was in store for all of the students. In class one day, Stewart Dinnen, the director of the training school, announced that the students were about to undergo an exercise in trusting God.

"The rules are quite simple," Stewart said. "Each of you will be given a one-pound note. With the money you are to undertake a month-long missionary tour of Scotland. You will be expected to pay all of your costs from the one pound, and when you get back to school after a month, you are to pay back that one pound. But during the time you are away, you are not allowed to take up a collection, and you cannot mention your needs to anyone. This is an experiment in trusting God to supply your needs, and you must not manipulate the experiment in any way. If you do, the experiment will be a failure."

Andrew was ready for the challenge, and soon afterward he and four other young men from the school set out to tour Scotland, preaching and witnessing as they went. They spoke in churches and halls along the way, always being careful not to mention their needs. As they traveled, though Andrew did not know how it happened, the five young men always had enough money to cover their costs. Sometimes one of the members of the team would receive a letter from home with money inside. At other times the men would receive letters containing money from people who had heard them preach along the way. Often these letters had notes in them that said, "I know you don't need money, because you would have said so. However, I just feel that God wants me to send you this amount." When they received money in this way, the team was careful to tithe on what they had received.

At still other times people would arrive out of the blue and give the men produce and other farm products. While the men were staying in a small town in the Scottish Highlands, someone arrived at the door with six hundred eggs. Andrew and his teammates ate eggs for breakfast, lunch, and dinner for several days, and they gave hundreds of them away as well.

Finally, after crisscrossing Scotland for a month, Andrew's team headed back to Glasgow. Upon their arrival at the WEC training school, they each paid back their one-pound note. Not only that, but they also had an extra ten pounds, which they handed over to the support of WEC missionaries.

Andrew was delighted to be back in Glasgow, but as he thought back over the experience of the previous month, he realized that he had learned much about trusting God to supply his needs. During the time they were gone, he and his teammates had eaten every day and had had a place to sleep each night and clothes to wear. And all that while they gave away ten percent of everything they received. *When you are about the King's business, He truly does provide,* Andrew told himself.

Before Andrew knew it, his first year at the training school was over. At the end of that year, a big graduation service was held for all of the second-year students, many of whom left for the mission field right away. After his graduation, Kees booked a ticket to Korea and promised to keep in touch with Andrew.

Andrew's second year at the training school sped by even faster than the first, and before he knew it, it was springtime. Even though his time at school was almost over, Andrew still had no idea what he should do next. He had faith, however, that God would send him a clear direction at the right time. The last place he expected to find this direction was in the basement of the school. He had gone to the basement to retrieve his suitcase, but as he reached for it, he noticed a glossy magazine lying on top it. Andrew had never seen the magazine before, and he had no idea how or why it had been left there. But when he picked up the magazine and flipped through its pages, what he saw and read on those pages was to forever change the course of his life.

Chapter 11

Behind the Iron Curtain

Andrew stood in the dingy basement, transfixed by the images he saw on the pages he was flipping through. The magazine was filled with the faces of bright, smiling young people—Chinese, Russians, and Poles. In the text that accompanied the photographs Andrew read that ninety-six million people had found peace, hope, and freedom in their lives and cooperation in their communities through the wonderful new world of socialism.

Socialism! Communism! How can these people be so duped? Andrew thought. The magazine was filled with articles about a better world, but Andrew didn't buy a word of it. As he thought about the Communists he had known, he certainly did not think that they held the key to a better world. He recalled one woman in particular. This woman, an avowed Communist, had worked with Andrew at the chocolate factory in Alkmaar. She was the most joyless, cynical person Andrew had ever known. She could hardly keep a scowl off her face, and she deeply resented the prayer groups and evangelistic outings that Andrew planned for the workers. Once she had told Andrew that God was the "invention of the exploiter class," and according to her, the wages that she and the other workers received for their labor were slave wages. And when Andrew had told her that he was leaving the factory, she looked him in the eye and said, "Yes, but the lies you've told are not leaving. You have hypnotized these people with your talk of salvation and pie in the sky. You've completely blinded them." That woman had nothing in common with the smiling, shiny-faced young people in the magazine.

As Andrew was about to put the magazine down and pick up his suitcase, something in the magazine caught his eye. It was a half-page advertisement, an invitation to be part of a giant youth festival being held in Warsaw in July. "Everyone Welcome" the advertisement read. *Everyone! I bet they don't want any Christian young people like me there,* Andrew chuckled to himself. But as the words crossed his mind, a strange compulsion overcame him. Somehow he knew he had to write to the address in the advertisement and ask if they would be willing to send him the visa materials and passes to go to the youth festival.

Knowing that Communists did not like or welcome Christians, Andrew decided not to hide his reasons for wanting to attend the youth festival. He wrote a straightforward letter, stating that he would like to hear firsthand the Communist point of view and explain his own Christian perspective. He dropped the letter into the mail that night, not knowing what kind of response, if any, he would get.

Within two weeks Andrew had received a reply. Yes, the letter he received said, the organizers of the youth festival would love to have Andrew come and listen to the superior ideology of Communism, and he was welcome to debate Christianity with anyone as well. The letter also informed him that a special train was leaving from Amsterdam for Warsaw and that because he was a student, he could get a discount on his train fare. And as if that were not surprising enough, identification passes fell out of the opened envelope.

The letter was all the guidance Andrew needed. As soon as the training school was over, Andrew headed back to Holland to prepare for his trip to Warsaw, Poland. On the way to Holland he stopped in to visit Mr. and Mrs. Hopkins in Kent. When he explained his new direction to them, at first Uncle Hoppy was shocked. "But you can't go behind the Iron Curtain, can you, lad?" he asked.

The *Iron Curtain* was a term made famous by British Prime Minister Winston Churchill, who used it to signify the line that separated the West from the countries of Eastern Europe, where the Soviet

Union had established puppet governments at the end of World War II. Traveling in these countries was very difficult, since visas were hard to come by. And travel there could also be dangerous, especially for Christians. Most Communist leaders seemed to be paranoid about outside information and influences in their countries, especially when it came to matters like religion, which they saw as a challenge to their authority and as undermining Communist values.

"I don't know why I can't go behind the Iron Curtain. I've been invited, and I've been honest about why I want to go," Andrew replied.

Uncle Hoppy nodded his head thoughtfully. "In that case let me be the first one who blesses you on your journey," he said. With that he reached into the pocket of his threadbare coat and pulled out a wad of five-pound notes. He counted off some of them and handed them to Andrew. "This should get you on the way," he said, handing over the notes. "Be sure you keep in touch, now."

Holding the five-pound notes in his hand, Andrew stood speechless. Uncle Hoppy was truly one of the most remarkable men he had ever met.

Back in Holland Andrew found Sint Pancras as he had left it. Time seemed to stand still there. He had one week at home to see everyone and pack for his trip to Poland. He made a hurried round of visits to Kees's family, Miss Meekle, who was amazed by the "strange" English he could now speak, and the workers at the chocolate factory. The Whetstras also were in the process of packing. They were moving to Amsterdam so that they could expand their flower-export business.

During the week Andrew also took the bus to Ermelo to visit his brother Ben and his wife. They were doing well, but Andrew had to gulp back tears when Ben told him that Thile had married a local baker in Gorkum. Any hopes he had of reconciling with her were dashed. But as he rode the bus back to Sint Pancras, Andrew came to the conclusion that Thile's marriage was probably for the best. He was twenty-seven years old now, and he had even less to offer a bride than he had before going off to train in Scotland. Still, he hoped that one day he would find a wife, though he realized she would have to be a very special woman to enter into a partnership with him.

On the morning of July 15, 1955, Andrew made his way to the railway station in Amsterdam. He lugged with him a heavy bag. He had packed the barest minimum of clothes and filled the rest of the bag with copies of a thirty-one-page booklet titled *The Way of Salvation* in Polish and a number of other European languages. He was aware that Karl Marx had once said, "Give me twenty-six lead soldiers and I will conquer the world." By this Marx was referring to the twenty-six letters of the alphabet cast in lead that were used to set type on a printing press to print literature. Andrew had decided to play the Communists at their own game, using literature to help spread the gospel behind the Iron Curtain.

When he reached the station in the heart of Amsterdam, Andrew was surprised by the size of the crowd of young people waiting for the train. He had expected perhaps fifty people at most to be heading to the youth festival, but several hundred people were lined up on the station platform. When the train pulled up beside the platform, the people surged aboard for the trip to Warsaw. Andrew lugged his heavy bag aboard, stowed it on a luggage rack, and found a seat for the journey.

In the evening, as the summer sun was beginning to set, the train pulled into the station in Warsaw. Once the group had arrived, they were met by guides who took them to their "hotel," which turned out to be a school building that had been converted into a dormitory for the youth festival. Andrew was shown to a math classroom, where thirty beds were laid out side by side.

That night one of the guides explained to the newly arrived group that over thirty thousand young people would be in Warsaw for the three-week-long festival. The guide then explained that in the mornings they would be loaded onto buses for sightseeing tours of the city and in the afternoons and evenings they would listen to inspiring speeches from a range of Communist leaders.

To Andrew this did not sound like a very exciting way to spend a day, but the next morning he boarded one of the sightseeing buses that pulled up in front of the school building. As the buses ferried the young people through the streets of Warsaw, even Andrew had to admit that what they were seeing was very impressive. The sightseers were shown new schools, factories that throbbed with the sound of machinery turning out all sorts of manufactured goods, blocks of apartment buildings that towered over the city, and shops that overflowed with things to buy.

After two days of sightseeing and listening to tedious speeches by grim-faced men and women, Andrew decided he wanted to see Warsaw for himself. He wondered what the city was like beyond the facade they were being shown from their sightseeing buses. Early one morning he got up and dressed before anyone else and hurried down the stairs and out the front door of the school building. For the rest of the day he wandered up and down the streets of Warsaw.

What Andrew saw as he walked shocked and dismayed him. Ten years after the end of World War II, whole blocks of the city were still in ruins from German and Russian bombs. Many of the people he saw were dressed in threadbare, ragged clothes, and at meat markets and vegetable stands, long lines of customers waited to buy food. The Warsaw he was seeing bore no resemblance to the gleaming Warsaw he had been shown from the sightseeing buses.

As if things could not get any worse, Andrew turned onto a rubble-strewn side street. All the buildings on this street had been reduced to rubble by the bombing. But much to Andrew's surprise, people still lived on the street. Like rabbits they had burrowed down through the rubble and set up homes in the basements of the bombed-out buildings. As he walked along, Andrew noticed a young girl playing amid the rubble and debris. He took one of the copies of *The Way of Salvation* in Polish that he had with him and handed it to her. She took the booklet and scampered away.

Moments later two heads appeared from amid a pile of rubble. A man and a woman, followed by the young girl, clambered out of the opening that led to their warren below ground. They were all dressed in filthy rags, and the man held up the booklet Andrew had given his daughter and shook his head. Andrew tried to talk to the man first in English, then in Dutch, and finally in the fractured German he still remembered from the Nazi occupation of Holland. But the man understood none of it. He just held up the booklet and shook his head. Then it dawned on Andrew that the man was trying to indicate that he could not read. Andrew gestured for the man to keep the booklet and walked on. He had stumbled onto a part of Warsaw that he was sure the Communist government had not intended for him to see.

As he walked, Andrew noticed a curious thing. He had come expecting to find the doors to the churches shut and barred, but instead he walked past Catholic and Protestant churches alike and found them open. He decided that he would attend one of the churches on Sunday.

Back in his dormitory room that night, Andrew sat depressed at all he had seen that day. Meanwhile

Hans, a Dutch Communist who slept in the same dormitory room, talked on enthusiastically about the achievements of Communism.

Andrew could share none of Hans's enthusiasm, and finally he said, "Hans, why don't you skip tomorrow's tour and speeches and go and see Warsaw for yourself. Go into the streets and see the things I saw today." He then gave Hans directions to some of the most shocking parts of the city.

The following evening Andrew found Hans sitting dejected in their dorm room. Hans explained to Andrew that he had taken his advice and gone to see the city for himself. "Andrew, I am leaving on the midnight train for home," Hans declared. "What I saw today scared me more than I have ever been scared in my life. I have to get out of this place."

On Sunday Andrew found his way to a Reformed church, where a service was already in progress. He slipped into a seat at the back of the sanctuary and was surprised by the size of the congregation: the church was three-quarters full. The singing was enthusiastic, and although he could not understand the sermon, since it was in Polish, Andrew believed it to be Bible based, judging by the way the pastor held up his Bible and read from it.

At the end of the service, the pastor came up to Andrew and spoke to him in English. Andrew expressed his surprise that Christians were allowed to worship so freely. In the West, he explained, all they had heard was how the Communist authorities had closed seminaries and arrested pastors. The pastor nodded and explained that they were allowed to worship freely so long as they stayed away from addressing political matters. "Yes, it is a compromise," the pastor noted, "but what can we do?"

Andrew nodded.

"Tell me, what church do you belong to at home?" the pastor asked.

"A Baptist church," Andrew replied.

"Then perhaps you would like to attend a Baptist church here in Warsaw?"

Andrew nodded again.

With that the pastor took a piece of paper and wrote down the address of a Baptist church and handed it to Andrew. "They will be having a service this evening," he said.

That evening Andrew found his way to the address the pastor had written down and slipped into the back of the service already in progress. His entry did not go unnoticed, however. People began to turn and look at him. Andrew decided that his clothes gave away the fact that he was a foreigner. On learning that a foreigner was in their midst, the pastor invited Andrew to come to the platform and speak to them.

Andrew walked to the front and asked whether anyone in the congregation spoke either English or German. A woman acknowledged that she spoke German, and Andrew invited her to the front. Then, in German, he spoke to the congregation, stopping after every sentence or two to let the woman translate his German into Polish.

When Andrew had finished speaking, the pastor stepped forward. "We want to thank you," he said. "Even if you had not said a word, just seeing you and having you here means so much to us. At times we think that we are all alone in our struggle."

Andrew was deeply touched by the pastor's words and by the warmth extended to him from the congregation.

During the next week, Andrew decided to go out into the streets of Warsaw and distribute copies of *The Way of Salvation* to the people who passed by. He stood on street corners, passing out the booklet, and much to his surprise, nearly everyone he offered a copy to took it. At first when he saw soldiers coming, Andrew would hurry away to another street corner. But then one day he asked himself why he was so scared of the soldiers. Why did he creep away when he saw them coming? After all, soldiers needed to hear the gospel as well. So when he noticed a group of soldiers approaching one day, he decided to stand his ground. The soldiers walked up to him, and he offered them each a copy of the booklet. They took the booklets and looked them over.

"I'm Dutch," Andrew said in German.

"Dutch," one of the soldiers replied in German.

But before Andrew could get a conversation started with the soldiers, their superior officer approached, and the soldiers quickly moved on, each grasping his copy of *The Way of Salvation.*

"So what do we have here?" the commanding officer asked in German.

Andrew handed the officer a copy of the booklet, and with a scowl on his face, the officer looked it over. Andrew's heart thumped as he waited to see whether he had perhaps gone too far. Would the officer arrest him or let him go?

After several minutes of looking over the booklet, the officer began asking questions about it. For the next two hours Andrew and the officer talked about the message of the booklet. When the officer finally walked away, Andrew was glad that he had confronted his fears and reached out to the soldiers. He was sure that the booklets would have an effect on them.

By the end of the week, Andrew had handed out all the copies of *The Way of Salvation* he had brought with him.

On the following Sunday Andrew once again found a church to attend. While at the service, he was surprised to learn that there was a shop in Warsaw that sold Bibles. He got the address, and on Monday he set out to find the store.

Andrew walked through the streets of Warsaw until he came to the address on New World Street. He stepped into the small shop and looked around while a man served a customer at the front of the store. A range of editions of the Bible were laid out on the shelves. Some were large editions, with the words of Jesus marked in red ink, and some were small editions, like the New Testament Andrew carried in his pocket. When the customer finally left the store, Andrew stepped up to the counter and spoke to the man behind it. "Good morning," he said in Polish.

The man responded in Polish, but since good morning was all the Polish Andrew knew, he asked in English, "Do you speak either German or English?"

"English," the man said.

Andrew expressed his surprise at finding a store selling Bibles in a Communist country. "Are there Bible bookshops in other Communist countries?" he asked.

Andrew noticed that the man was guarded in his response. The man's eyes darted back and forth as the man made sure before he spoke that no one else was in the store. "Some yes, some no," the man replied.

After a long silence, the man went on. This time his voice was not much above a whisper, and Andrew had to lean in to hear what the man was saying.

"I understand that in Russia Bibles are very scarce," the man said. "Fortunes are being made there with Bibles. A man will smuggle ten Bibles into Russia and sell them for enough money to buy a motorcycle. He drives the motorcycle here to Poland or East Germany and sells it for profit. He then uses the profit to buy more Bibles that he smuggles into Russia and sells for a fortune, and so the cycle goes."

The man's words deeply impacted Andrew, and as he walked back to the mathematics classroom dormitory, Andrew pondered those words. People were smuggling Bibles into the Soviet Union for profit. But was anyone smuggling Bibles into that country for love, for the love of Jesus Christ, and the love of seeing the gospel spread there?

Finally the last day of the three-week-long youth festival arrived. The day was to be marked by the Parade of Triumph, a large march through the streets of Warsaw by the festival participants. However, Andrew decided to forego the event. It was his last day in Poland, and he wanted to spend the time praying for the people he had spoken with and given copies of *The Way of Salvation* to during his stay in Warsaw, as well as for the Polish people in general.

Andrew was up early that morning. The sun was just climbing above the horizon to the east as he walked out into the street. He walked to one of the city's broad avenues and found a bench to sit on. As the golden rays of the sun warmed him, Andrew pulled the small New Testament from his pocket and laid it on his knee. He reflected on his time in Warsaw. On the three Sundays he had been in the city, he had attended a number of Protestant, Catholic, and Orthodox churches, where he had been warmly received. He had handed out hundreds of copies of *The Way of Salvation* in the streets and had talked to countless people, both those attending the youth festival and the citizens of Warsaw, about the gospel. Now he felt it was time to pray for those people, to pray that God would strengthen the Christians he had had fellowship with and stir the hearts of those he had shared the gospel with. Andrew flipped open the New Testament on his knee, placed his hand on it, and began to pray.

Andrew was unsure how long he had been praying when he noticed the sound of music in the distance. The music grew louder, and as he looked down the avenue, he saw that the Parade of Triumph was approaching. Soon a column of young people eight abreast was marching past. The paraders sang loudly and shouted slogans at the top of their voices. Andrew looked at them. These were the evangelists of Communism. But where were the evangelists for Jesus Christ behind the Iron Curtain? As far as Andrew was aware, WEC had never sent a missionary behind the Iron Curtain. And he was sure that that was probably the case for other denominations and mission organizations in the West.

As he thought about this, Andrew looked down at the New Testament on his knee. The book was opened to Revelation, chapter three, and he read the verse beside his index finger that was holding the book open. It was the second verse of the chapter, and the words seemed to leap out at him: "Awake, and strengthen what remains and is on the point of death."

The words startled Andrew, and before he realized it, tears were streaming down his cheeks. Was God speaking to him? "Is this what You are saying to me, Lord?" Andrew prayed. "Are You telling me that my life's work is here behind the Iron Curtain, strengthening what remains?"

It was a crazy idea. Andrew knew it. How could one young, unsupported Dutchman make a difference in such a large mission field? But no matter how he tried to dismiss the idea, Andrew could not get rid of the feeling that God was speaking to him about his future. He was still pondering this when he climbed aboard the train late that afternoon for the journey back to Holland. Was God really giving him direction for his future ministry?

Chapter 12

The Cup of Suffering

Unlike his return from Indonesia, when Andrew got home from Poland to Sint Pancras, this time everyone in the village wanted to hear about his experiences. This was a pleasant surprise, and within a week of arriving back, Andrew had talked at several house meetings in the village about all the things he had heard, seen, and done while in Warsaw. Soon invitations began arriving from as far away as Amsterdam for him to come and talk about the "suffering church behind the Iron Curtain." Andrew protested that he was not any kind of expert on the subject, but Christians were eager to hear what he had to say anyway. After all, they told him, he had seen and heard much more than they had.

Andrew's family was also supportive of him. In the time he had been way at the WEC training school, his family had built above the garden shed another room, which Mr. van der Bijl had moved in to. The room Andrew's father had vacated was the biggest room in the house. It had always been a bedroom, and Andrew assumed that his sister Geltje and her husband, Arie, would want it. But they did not. Instead they told Andrew that he should move into the room. They had decided that he could use it not only as his bedroom but also as the headquarters for his ministry.

Andrew was humbled by Geltje and Arie's gesture. He was also a little concerned. It seemed to him that everyone else thought that he knew what he was going to do with his life. After all, he had speaking engagements and a "headquarters," and he had been asked to write a series of magazine articles on Communism and Christianity—and all of this because he had gone to Poland for three weeks to attend a youth festival. Other people might have confidence that he knew where he was headed, but the truth was, Andrew had no real idea what God wanted him to do next. He was sure that God had spoken to him during his last day in Warsaw, but since he had no idea how this calling might work out, Andrew decided he should just keep taking the next opportunity that presented itself and pray that God would show him the way.

And that is what happened, though not in a way that Andrew could have predicted. Just as he finished speaking to a large crowd in Amsterdam, a stout woman made a beeline toward him. Andrew recognized the woman instantly. She had led the Dutch contingent to the youth festival in Warsaw. She planted herself firmly in front of him and got straight to the point. "I don't approve of what you said tonight," she announced.

"I didn't think you would," Andrew replied.

"You emphasized the things in postrevolutionary countries that we Communists are still trying to change. You should look to the future and realize that we offer many advantages for today's youth," the woman said.

"I only spoke about what I saw with my own eyes and the experiences I had," Andrew shrugged.

The woman pounced on this statement. "That is the point. You need to see more so that you will be able to speak more positively. I am in charge of organizing a group of fifteen people for a fact-finding trip into Czechoslovakia. We'll be gone for a month. We have educators and communicators, and we need someone with a church perspective. Would you like to come?"

Andrew shook his head. He barely had enough money for the bus fare home to Sint Pancras, let alone enough for a second trip behind the Iron Curtain. "I don't have the money," he replied.

The woman looked him up and down with a shrewd look on her face. "I'll work out the money. If you want to come, say so," she snapped.

Andrew looked at her. Was she really offering him a free trip to Czechoslovakia? "And you'll deal with the visas?" he asked.

"Everything is already taken care of. What do you say? Are you coming?"

"When do we leave?" Andrew smiled.

As he rode home on the bus that night, Andrew could hardly believe what had just taken place. He was off on a second trip behind the Iron Curtain. Was this just a coincidence, or was God up to something big?

On a cold November morning, three months after his visit to Warsaw, Andrew found himself standing in Prague, rain pouring down as he listened to their tour guide explaining about yet another wonderful achievement of Communism. He had been in Czechoslovakia for three weeks now, and every day had followed much the same pattern. Andrew and the fourteen other members of the party were herded from one staged event to another while their tour guide expounded on the virtues of Communism and pointed out how much freer the Czech people were now than they had ever been in the past. Andrew doubted this, but it was hard to find any evidence to disprove it. The tour leader, the stout Dutch woman who had recruited Andrew for the trip, kept a particularly sharp eye on him, making sure that he was usually at the front of the group, and counted to make sure that everyone was present and accounted for at least once an hour. She said that it was to make sure no one got lost, but Andrew was convinced that she was worried about his going off and exploring Prague alone. He wished he could, but he did not see how he could do it.

In the meantime, the tour guide offered Andrew an official look at the "harmonious cooperation" between the church and the government. "The government does not wish to interfere with religious beliefs," she told him. "In fact, it has an entire facility dedicated to producing a new and improved version of the Bible. Would you like to visit it?"

"Of course," Andrew replied.

The next day Andrew and the tour guide set out for the center of Prague to a large office building called the Interchurch Center. The guide explained that the building was the center for all the Protestant churches in the country. Inside the building, Andrew and the guide wound their way through a maze of gloomy corridors until they came to a large room. Inside sat a number of scholars clad in black coats, some of them almost hidden by the piles of papers and books stacked on their desks. Andrew spoke to one of the scholars in German. "May I see the new translation?" he asked.

The scholar got up and walked to another desk. He returned moments later. Andrew had expected to be handed a bound copy of the new Bible, but instead the scholar handed him a typed manuscript, its pages dog-eared from constant handling.

"The translation hasn't been published yet?" Andrew asked.

"No, not yet," the scholar replied, and Andrew noted the sadness in his eyes as he answered. "We've had the translation finished since the war, but..."

"The scholars are now working on a Bible dictionary," the tour guide interrupted.

Sheepishly the scholar looked at the tour guide and then down at his desk.

"Is the Bible dictionary ready yet?" Andrew asked.

"Almost," the scholar replied.

"But what good will a Bible dictionary do if there are no Bibles? Are there earlier translations of the Bible available?" Andrew shot back.

The Bible scholar was silent for a moment, and then quickly he blurted, "No. It is difficult, very difficult to find Bibles in Czechoslovakia these days."

With that the tour guide ended the visit and led Andrew out of the Interchurch Center building.

Andrew was very quiet at dinner that night. He was thinking about how shrewd the Communists were. Instead of openly banning the Bible, they had announced that they were producing a better version. But that better version would never be published. As he thought about it, Andrew became frustrated. Tomorrow, Sunday, would be his last full day in Czechoslovakia, and he had not yet been able to find a way to talk privately with any Christians. He decided that one way or another he was going to find a way to do just that.

The following morning the group set out on yet another bus tour of important revolutionary sites. Predictably the tour guide had the bus stop at each site while she explained why the particular place had played such an important role in the Communist takeover of the country. By the second stop, Andrew had managed to position himself at the very back of the bus, desperately looking for some way to escape from the group.

As he sat in the back, his eyes rested on the rear door to his left. The door had a faulty hinge, which left about a twelve-inch gap at the side when it was closed. Twelve inches. Andrew sucked in his breath. Could he squeeze through a twelve-inch gap? Yes! He was sure he could. He sat patiently at the back as the tour bus drove on. At each intersection he waited for the gaze of everyone to be directed toward the front, but there was always someone looking at a sight to the rear. Then finally the bus pulled up to a bronze statue of a man on horseback.

The tour guide launched into an impassioned speech about the statue's significance. Everyone peered at the statue—everyone, that is, except Andrew, who saw his chance, slipped quietly from his seat, and moved toward the faulty door. Andrew took one last look at his fellow passengers, who were all listening intently to the tour guide. He let out his breath and squeezed through the gap in the door. He felt the road beneath his feet and managed to pull the rest of his body through the opening just before the bus belched a plume of blue exhaust smoke and drove on.

For the first time on the tour, Andrew was alone in Czechoslovakia. He looked around. He was sure that he had seen a church nearby on a previous bus tour through this part of the city. He reasoned that it was probably to the east, and he set out walking in that direction. Sure enough, ten minutes later he was seated in the back row of a church. As the congregation stood to sing a hymn, Andrew noticed something interesting that made him wonder whether everyone in the building was farsighted. Those people with hymnals were holding them up high at arm's length. Other people were doing the same with notebooks.

After a few minutes, Andrew figured out that the people weren't all farsighted after all. Because hymnals were in such sort supply, whoever was lucky enough to own one held it in such a way that as many people as possible could see the words to the hymns. Also, on the pages of the notebooks held aloft, people had copied the words of the hymns by hand. And when the pastor quoted Bible references during his sermon, the few people who owned Bibles held them up in the same way for people to see. Andrew suddenly realized how precious the small Dutch Bible in his pocket was—and how precious the freedom to own one at will.

At the end of the service Andrew shook the pastor's hand and said quietly, "Brother, I am a believer from Holland. I'm here to meet with Christians in your country."

"Please come and talk with me, brother. You are the first believer we have met from the West in many years," the pastor said.

A short while later Andrew was seated in the pastor's apartment, sipping coffee and listening to what the pastor had to say.

"Things here are difficult. The government is trying to gain a stranglehold on the church. They are even choosing the theological students. Only those who support the regime are allowed to study theology. And as a pastor I have to renew my license every two months. All pastors must do this, and recently a friend of mine had his request for a renewal turned down. The government did not tell him why. They don't have to." The pastor drank a mouthful of coffee and then continued. "And even with a license we are not free to preach what we wish. We must write out each sermon ahead of time and have it approved by the government before we can preach it."

Andrew did not quite know how to respond to this information. He just let out a gentle whistle.

"We are going to have another service soon, brother. I would like you to come and speak to us," the pastor said.

"But I thought sermons had to be approved ahead of time," Andrew inquired.

"I am not asking you to *preach*," the pastor said with a twinkle in his eye. "I want you to bring us 'greetings' from the Christians in your country. And if you wish, you could also bring us 'greetings' from the Lord Jesus."

And that is what Andrew did. With the help of a young medical student named Antonin, who served as his translator, Andrew gave the people a brief greeting from the Christians in Holland and the West. Then he spent the next thirty minutes giving the people greetings from Jesus Christ. Those in the congregation so appreciated his words that they gathered around to shake his hand at the end of the service.

This approach was so successful that Andrew and Antonin spent the rest of the afternoon presenting greetings to four other Czech churches. The final church they visited was a Moravian church on the other side of Prague. About one hundred people were gathered in the sanctuary, and Andrew was surprised that about forty of these were young people between the ages of eighteen and twenty-five.

At the end of this service, after Andrew had presented his greetings, a number of the young people gathered around Andrew and peppered him with questions. They found it hard to believe that Christians in Holland and the West were not penalized for being Christians. They explained that to be a Christian in Czechoslovakia meant being treated like a second-class citizen. The Czech government would not allow Christians to hold good jobs or attend university. For these young people, being a Christian meant having to endure a good deal of suffering.

As the conversation was winding down, one of the Moravians handed Antonin a silver lapel pin. "They want you to have this as a gift of remembrance," Antonin explained to Andrew.

Andrew looked at the lapel pin, which was in the shape of a small cup. "What does the cup signify?" he asked.

"It is the symbol of the church in Czechoslovakia," Antonin said, attaching the pin to the lapel of Andrew's jacket. "We call it the Cup of Suffering."

One of the young Moravians then said something, and Antonin translated his words. "Now you are a partaker of the cup with us. When the people of Holland ask you about the cup, tell them about the Czech Christians. Remind them that we too are part of the Body of Christ. Tell them that we are in pain, that we are suffering."

Darkness had descended over Prague by the time Andrew said good-bye to Antonin and headed off to find the tour group. He wondered how the members of the group would have taken his disappearance. Surely, he told himself, nothing too bad could happen as a result of it.

When he got back to the hotel, the group was not there, nor were they at the restaurant where they had eaten most nights. Andrew ordered a sandwich there anyway, and he had just taken his first bite when the tour leader, the stout Dutch woman, strode into the room. Her face was bright red, and she kept her mouth firmly shut. She motioned for Andrew to follow her. Andrew got up from the table and followed her out the front door of the restaurant and into a waiting limousine. Not a word passed between them, and Andrew supposed she was too angry with him to speak.

He was right. Then just before they arrived back at the hotel, the woman could hold her peace no longer. "You have held us all up for half a day. We have looked everywhere for you, in all the hospitals, the police stations, even the morgue. And now I find you calmly eating a sandwich. Where have you been?" she exploded.

Andrew stuck his hands in his pockets so that she would not see him shaking. "Oh," he said as lightly as he could. "I got separated from you, so I decided to do a bit of exploring on my own. I had no idea I would cause this much trouble. I apologize."

"That's not enough," the woman snapped back. "You are officially unwelcome here ever again. I am sorry I brought you along on this trip. If you ever try to come back to this country, you will find your way blocked at the border. I will personally see to it."

Andrew stared out the window of the limousine. Had he gone astray somehow or was this all part of God's plan? He did not know.

Chapter 13

"Don't Take No for an Answer!"

Back in Sint Pancras Andrew felt lonelier than ever before. He had plenty to do to keep him busy. He had written to the embassies of various countries behind the Iron Curtain, including Yugoslavia and Hungary, asking for visas to travel there, but he never received the replies he sought. After being turned down so many times, he began to doubt whether he was even supposed to again reach out to people behind the Iron Curtain. Money was very tight too. Andrew was embarrassed that he could not contribute to the household income. All he could do was continue writing letters to people and embassies and pray.

Slowly Andrew's situation began to change. Andrew wrote an article about the plight of Christians in Communist countries. The article was published in a magazine, and as a result of its publication, several readers sent money to help Andrew with his mission. The amounts were small, but then so too were Andrew's needs: a Czech Bible for Antonin, his interpreter in Prague, and a new jacket.

Soon something else happened. Andrew received a letter from a man in Amersfoort whom he had never met. The man introduced himself as Karl de Graaf. He said that God had directed his prayer group to ask Andrew to come and speak to them. It all sounded a little strange to Andrew, but he decided to go anyway. Amersfoort was near Ermelo, and Andrew could visit his brother Ben while he was there.

The prayer meeting in Amersfoort was unlike any prayer meeting Andrew had ever been to. About a dozen men and women were gathered in the de Graafs' parlor. There was no Bible study first and no fixed focus for their prayer. Rather, people sat listening for God to speak to them about an issue, which often meant there were long periods of silence as they did this. When a person felt that God had spoken to him or her, he or she would pray out about it fervently. Andrew was amazed at some of the things people prayed about, but more than anything, he was struck by the fervency of the people and the love and commitment to each other and to God that he felt in the room. For Andrew the time at the prayer meeting seemed to fly by, and he was astounded to learn when the meeting finally ended that it was four thirty in the morning!

A week later, while Andrew was writing another article for the magazine, he heard a knock at the door. Much to his surprise it was Karl de Graaf. Karl got straight to the point. "Andrew, I have come to ask you a question. Do you know how to drive a car?"

Andrew's mind went back nearly nine years to when he had careened out of control in the Bren troop carrier. The thought of it made him want to laugh, but he could see that Karl was in a serious mood. "No, sir," he replied.

"Well, you need to learn. Last night when we were praying, God told us to tell you that it's very important to your future that you learn to drive and get a license," Karl said.

Andrew nodded. Then much to Andrew's amazement, Karl turned and left. "I am just the messenger," Karl said over his shoulder. "Learn to drive, Andrew."

Andrew did not give much thought to this two-minute interlude in his day, but he did wonder how on earth he would learn to drive. No one in the village had a car. In fact, the Whetstras were the only friends he knew with a motor vehicle, and they now lived in Amsterdam. There was no way he was going all that way so that they could give him driving lessons. The whole idea was just not realistic. However, a week later Karl was back.

"I didn't think you'd do anything about it," he told Andrew, shaking his head as if he were talking to a schoolboy. "Come on. I will teach you myself."

Andrew turned out to be a quick learner, and within a month he had a driver's license. Having a driver's license seemed a little ridiculous to him. He could not afford to buy himself a bicycle, let alone a car. But he had to admit that it felt good having the license in his pocket.

In the spring of 1956 the people of Hungary revolted against the puppet Communist government set up in their country by the Soviet Union at the end of World War II. Eventually Soviet tanks were sent to Hungary to restore order and prop up the government, although not before thousands of Hungarians had fled their country and crossed the border into Austria. These people lived in huge refugee camps near the border and were in desperate need of help. When word reached Holland of the needs of these refugees, Andrew was one of the first to agree to go and help. In fact, he was on the first bus to leave Holland for the refugee camps in Austria. He and several other volunteers crowded into the front of the bus because the rest of the bus was filled to the brim with the most-needed supplies—food, clothing, and medicine.

In Austria Andrew found the refugees living in deplorable conditions. Often up to twelve families were living on top of each other in a single building. The people were dirty, hungry, and dispirited. Andrew soon learned that it was not only Hungarians living in the camps. Thousands of refugees from Communist Yugoslavia were there as well, and in West Germany more refugee camps were packed with people who had fled from East Germany and Czechoslovakia.

As the volunteers distributed supplies and worked among the refugees, Andrew was surprised by the refugees' lack of knowledge about Christianity and, in particular, about the Bible. He began offering classes to teach the people the most elementary things about the Bible. Using interpreters, he taught those who attended day after day what the Bible said regarding God and how people could have a relationship with Him.

Andrew was astounded at the change this knowledge brought in the lives of the refugees who attended his classes. The years of despair etched into their faces slowly faded away, to be replaced with smiles, and the people's despair changed into hope.

The supplies the volunteers had taken with them were soon exhausted. Andrew returned home to Sint Pancras long enough to collect more food, clothing, medicine, and Bibles before heading back to West Germany and Austria to continue helping with the relief effort. The work was exhausting, but Andrew was glad that he could bring some comfort to these refugees who had lost everything.

Three weeks after returning with more supplies, Andrew received a telegram from his sister, informing him that their father had collapsed and died in his garden. Andrew was in West Berlin at the time, and he caught the first train home to Holland. Mr. van der Bijl's funeral service was simple and moving. The family house in Sint Pancras seemed empty now without Papa in it, and Andrew was glad to get back to his work among the refugees.

Andrew had learned that the refugee camps in West Berlin were not new, as were those camps holding Hungarians and Yugoslavians in Austria. The German refugee camps had existed since the end of World War II. They were filled with people who had lost everything in the war, and now the people seemed to have been forgotten by the world. Many children lived in the camps, having been born and raised there. And in a camp where two single people were allotted more space than a married couple, many of these children were illegitimate and often unparented.

Andrew worked hard to try to arrange for some of these refugee children to go to Holland, where families were willing to adopt them. However, the plan proved to be more difficult than Andrew had imagined. Before they could travel to Holland, the children needed to pass a medical examination. Unfortunately, tuberculosis had become an epidemic in the refugee camps. Virtually no one was living there who did not have the disease. As a result, the children failed the medical examination and could not be cleared for travel to the Netherlands.

As Andrew worked away one particularly busy day in the refugee camp, a strange thought passed through his mind. *Today you will get your visa to enter Yugoslavia.* Andrew did not know where the thought came from, but he waited eagerly for the morning mail to see whether it was true. Sure enough, there was an official-looking letter from the Yugoslavian consulate that his sister Geltje had sent on to him from Holland. Andrew eagerly opened the letter and read: "Your application for a visa has been denied."

Andrew stared at the words for a long time. They relayed the exact opposite of what he had expected to read. Was that really God's voice he had heard in his head earlier in the day, or was it his own imagination? As he thought about it, however, Andrew decided that it was a strange coincidence that after all these months of waiting, the visa rejection should arrive that very day. Then he heard the voice in his head again. *Don't take no for an answer!* it said.

Andrew sprang into action. "Today I will get that visa!" he said as he hurried up to his room to collect some passport-size headshots and change his clothes. He was off to the Yugoslavian embassy in West Berlin.

It was lunchtime when he arrived at the embassy, far too late to get any kind of attention on a normal day, but Andrew climbed the steps anyway. He sat down and once again filled out the paperwork necessary to apply for a visa, only this time he did not write the word *missionary* on the line next to "Occupation."

"What should I put, God?" he prayed silently.

The word *teacher* came to mind, and Andrew thought of the Bible verses that commanded believers to go into the world and teach all nations. Yes, it was not a lie to say that he was a teacher.

Much to Andrew's surprise, an official beckoned

him over to a desk. "Sit down here," he said, "and I will examine your application while you wait."

Andrew handed over his paperwork and sat nervously as the man looked through his application. After a few minutes, the man got up and walked away. Twenty minutes later he returned. "Here you are, Mr. van der Bijl. Thank you for waiting, and enjoy your visit to Yugoslavia," he said.

Just like that, Andrew had the visa he had been waiting for months to receive, and he received it on the same day he got a letter from the consulate in Holland rejecting his application. Completely stunned, Andrew returned to the hostel where he was staying near the refugee camp. He wanted to tell someone the good news, but the van der Bijl house in Sint Pancras did not have a telephone, so he decided to call the Whetstras in Amsterdam.

"Hello," the voice of Mr. Whetstra said on the other end of the telephone line.

"Hello, Mr. Whetstra. This is Andrew. I'm lucky to find you home in the afternoon," Andrew said.

"Andrew, nice to hear your voice. I thought you were in Berlin. We were sorry to hear of the passing of your father."

"Thank you, Mr. Whetstra. Yes, I am in Berlin. I have good news, and I wanted to tell someone. I have in my one hand a letter from the Yugoslavian consulate in Holland denying my visa request. I received the letter in the mail today. In my other hand I have my passport, stamped with a visa to enter Yugoslavia, issued by the Yugoslavian embassy here in Berlin today. I'm on my way behind the Iron Curtain again," Andrew said excitedly.

"That is good news, Andrew. You had better come home and get your keys."

"I'm sorry, Mr. Whetstra. Our connection must be bad. I thought you said keys."

"I did say keys, Andrew—the keys to your new Volkswagen. Mrs. Whetstra and I decided several months ago that if you got the visa, you would also get our car. So now you need to come home and pick up the keys to it," Mr. Whetstra said.

Andrew hung up the phone a little bewildered. How could he take the Whetstras' car? When he got back to Amsterdam, he tried his best to talk them out of their offer to give him the car. But the Whetstras would hear none of it.

"We've prayed about this, and we are sure that God told us to do this. The car is needed for the King's business, and we are honored to be able to provide it for you," Mr. Whetstra told Andrew as he handed over the keys.

Andrew gave in and took the keys, and the two men went down to the clerk's office to have the title to the car transferred.

Later that afternoon Andrew was driving along the polder road toward Sint Pancras, his hands firmly on the steering wheel of a nearly new blue Volkswagen. As he drove past the familiar landmarks, he knew what God wanted him to do next—

he was going to Yugoslavia, and he was going to drive there in his own car.

Andrew set himself a deadline of March 1957 to be at the Yugoslav border. In the meantime he had more articles to write for the Christian magazine. He had also hoped to personally contact at least one Christian in Yugoslavia before his trip, but this had proved impossible. The best he could do was write a letter to a man at a twelve-year-old address that the Dutch Bible Society had provided him with. Andrew had no way of knowing whether the man was alive or dead, let alone whether he was still at the address, but he wrote a vague letter explaining that he would like to get in touch with the man.

On a beautiful spring day in late March 1957, Andrew pulled to the side of the road in a tiny Austrian village, minutes from the Yugoslav border. This was his moment of reckoning. He had driven six hundred miles with a car full of Bibles and tracts in the Slovene and Croatian languages, and now he was about to cross the border into Yugoslavia. But the Yugoslav documents had been very clear and specific. General Tito, the leader of Yugoslavia, had decreed that anyone crossing the border into his country could bring with him or her only personal belongings. People coming into Yugoslavia could not carry anything to sell on the black market or to give away. And they were explicitly banned from carrying printed material into the country. Such printed material was considered foreign propaganda, and the person carrying it would be arrested on the spot.

Despite this warning, Andrew was certain that God had opened the door for him to make this trip. He had nowhere else to go except forward to the border. Andrew slipped the Volkswagen into gear and drove on. As he drove, he prayed out loud to himself, "Lord, my bag is full of Scriptures that I want to deliver to your children—my brothers and sisters across this border. When You walked this earth, You made the blind eyes see. Now I am asking You to make the seeing eyes blind. Don't let the guards see a single thing that they are not meant to see. Amen."

Just as Andrew finished his prayer, the Yugoslav border post came into view.

Chapter 14

Someone to Share His Life With

Andrew pulled his blue Volkswagen to a halt in front of the barrier that blocked the road. Two border guards emerged from the small guard-house beside the barrier. The guards seemed both delighted and surprised by Andrew's arrival, and Andrew supposed that his was the first car to stop at the border crossing that day. He rolled down the window, and in German one of the guards asked to see his passport. Andrew handed over his passport, and as the guard looked it over, the other guard asked him to step out of the car. Andrew did as he was asked, and the guard then began feeling around Andrew's camping gear. In the folds of the camping gear, Andrew had hidden boxes of tracts, and his heart rate increased as the guard ran his hands over the pile of equipment. "Lord, make seeing eyes blind," he prayed under his breath.

"Do you have anything to declare?" the first guard asked as he handed back Andrew's passport.

"I have some money, a wristwatch, a camera—"

"Please, take this suitcase out," the second guard said, cutting Andrew off. The guard had finished with the camping gear and now rested his hand on one of the suitcases in the back of the Volkswagen.

"Yes, certainly," Andrew said as he reached in and lifted out the suitcase, which he then laid on the ground beside the car and opened.

The guard moved several shirts aside, and there in plain view was a pile of gospel tracts. Andrew could feel the palms of his hands getting clammy. Again he prayed under his breath, "Lord, make seeing eyes blind."

"It seems very dry for this time of year," Andrew remarked to the other guard to break the tension he was feeling.

"Not for March," the guard replied. "Our rainy season is during the middle of summer."

"Is that right," Andrew responded. "In Holland September and October are our rainiest months."

"July is our wettest month," the guard said.

"July? No, not July. We get much more rain in August," chimed the guard inspecting the suitcase. The weather now seemed more important to the guard than the contents of Andrew's suitcase. The guard put the shirts back in place and closed the suitcase, and then the three men fell into a conversation about the weather. After they had been talking for several minutes, the guard who had been inspecting Andrew's suitcase asked, "So, do you have anything else to declare?"

"Only small things," Andrew answered.

"We don't bother with small things," the guard replied.

With that the other guard raised the barrier. Andrew loaded the suitcase back into the car and drove into Yugoslavia, giving a little wave to the two guards as he left. As he drove on, Andrew thanked God for allowing him to make it through the checkpoint with all of the Bibles.

Andrew's first stop in Yugoslavia was the city of Zagreb, where he had sent the letter. He found the address the Bible Society in Holland had furnished him and pulled the car to a halt in front of it. As he stepped out of the Volkswagen onto the sidewalk, a man walked up and asked him if he was a Dutchman.

"Yes," Andrew replied in German.

The man broke into a huge grin and started pumping Andrew's hand. "This is a miracle, this is a miracle!" he repeated. "I got your letter this morning, although I have not lived at this address for many years. I did not know what I should do, so I came here—not two minutes before you—and now I am talking to you. You are a Christian, right?"

Andrew nodded and invited the man, whose name was Jamil, to ride with him in the car. As the Volkswagen purred along, Jamil thanked Andrew many times for coming.

"Just knowing that Christians on the outside care means so much," Jamil said. "We all feel so isolated, so alone here."

Andrew asked Jamil whether he knew of someone who could serve as an interpreter during his visit. Jamil suggested a devout engineering student named Nikola. The two men drove to Nikola's apartment, and Nikola immediately agreed to help Andrew in any way he could.

That night Andrew marveled at what an amazing day it had been. God had somehow stopped the guards from seeing any of the banned literature he was carrying into the country, guided him to a Christian contact, and provided an interpreter for his visit. He could hardly wait to get up the following morning and see what would happen next.

Andrew's visa allowed him to stay in Yugoslavia for fifty days, and Andrew got maximum use out of each of those days. He held about one hundred meetings throughout the country, sometimes preaching up to six times on Sundays in churches both in tiny villages and in large cities. Everywhere he went, Christians were eager to learn about what was happening outside of Yugoslavia, as well as what was happening to Christians in other parts of the country. Andrew observed that the Christians in the north of Yugoslavia had more freedom than those in the south and that the Communists were leaving the old people alone but trying everything they could to dissuade the children and young people from believing in "fairytales and Bible myths."

Sometimes the police took down the names of people who were attending the meetings where Andrew spoke, and Andrew would hear later that some of these people had been arrested or lost their jobs. But it seemed to Andrew that despite the obvious danger, more and more people were at each new meeting.

On May 1, 1957, Andrew and Nikola drove into Belgrade, the capital and largest city in Yugoslavia. The Communist May Day celebration was well under way by the time they arrived, and the city was brimming with people. The hotels and restaurants were full to capacity, and Andrew thought that he and Nikola would have to sleep in the car for the night. However, they made contact with a local pastor, who invited them to stay in his apartment. The following evening Andrew spoke at the pastor's church.

When he arrived at the church, Andrew found the place filled to the brim with well-dressed, urbane people. After the pastor introduced him, Andrew stood on the platform and began to tell the crowd stories from the gospels. After he had said a few sentences, he would stop and let Nikola translate his words into Serbo-Croatian. As he spoke, Andrew noticed a banging sound. He wondered for a moment whether it was the secret police breaking their way into the building to arrest him and those in the congregation. However, moments later he saw that the banging was coming from the side of the sanctuary where several men had removed a door so that the people who had overflowed into the choir room next door could see and hear him speak.

After presenting the gospel, Andrew then asked those in the room to raise their hand if they wanted to commit their life to Christ or renew a previous commitment to Him. To his surprise every person present raised his or her hand. Andrew decided that the people must have misunderstood him, and he asked Nikola to explain the serious step they were taking. Then he made a second appeal, this time asking those in the room who wanted to commit themselves to following Jesus Christ to stand. Everyone in the room stood.

Amazed at the response of the people, Andrew began to talk to them about the need to pray each day as new Christians. Andrew noticed many faces light up around the room at this suggestion. But when he told them that they would also need to read and study their Bibles each day, he seemed to lose the attention of the audience. People fidgeted in their seats and were no longer looking at him. Confused, Andrew asked the pastor what the problem was.

"Prayer, yes, that we can do each day," the pastor replied. "In fact, I like what you said about the need to pray. But reading the Bible... Brother Andrew, most of the people in this room do not have Bibles."

Since Belgrade was such a cosmopolitan city, Andrew had expected most of the people who attended the meeting to own Bibles. "How many of you own Bibles?" he asked.

Only seven hands went up. Only seven people out of all those in attendance had Bibles, and Andrew had already distributed the Bibles he smuggled into Yugoslavia. Later that evening Andrew and the pastor worked out a plan whereby the seven Bibles could be shared among the members of the congregation for individual reading and for studying in small groups.

That night as he lay in bed in the pastor's apartment and thought about the situation with the Bibles, Andrew felt pricked in his heart. In the West anybody could buy and own a Bible. Why, many people owned two or three in different translations or versions. But this was not so behind the Iron Curtain. Andrew prayed and promised God that he would do whatever he could to help alleviate the situation. He promised that when he could get ahold of Bibles in the languages of the people behind the Iron Curtain, he would smuggle the Bibles to the people.

Andrew was sad when his fifty days were up and he had to leave Yugoslavia, yet he left the country with a clear sense of calling. It was clear to him that God wanted him to smuggle Bibles into Communist countries and distribute them to weary Christians. But this mission was so different from anything else Andrew had ever heard of that it made him feel very alone. As he drove back toward the Netherlands, he began to wish that he had at least one person who shared his strange calling—a wife perhaps? "Yes, a wife is just what I need. I will be thirty next year, and I would love to have a wife to share my life with," he told himself.

After he arrived back in Sint Pancras, Andrew continued to think about how amazing it would be to have a wife to share his calling and mission. Then one day, in the middle of his morning prayer time, the answer began to unfold. Suddenly Andrew saw before him the face of a woman named Corrie van Dam. Corrie was a pretty, blonde young woman who had worked at the chocolate factory with him five years before.

Andrew had always been impressed with Corrie's Christian faith and warm personality, two things he was sure would have attracted her a husband long before now. Still, he had to know for certain whether she was married or not, so he took his father's old bicycle and rode into Alkmaar. During the years that Andrew had worked at the chocolate factory, Corrie's parents had often welcomed the workers into their home for coffee and cake after a youth rally. As a result, Andrew knew the way to the van Dam house—or at least to what had once been the van Dam home. When he arrived there, he learned that the family had moved to Amsterdam. As far as the new occupants of the house knew, Corrie was just finishing up her nursing training, and they thought that she was not married.

Andrew's hopes soared as he drove the Volkswagen into Amsterdam. He found his way to the van Dams' new address and knocked on the door to their house. Upon opening the door, Mrs. van

Dam was delighted to see Andrew. Andrew soon learned that Mr. van Dam was very ill and that Mrs. van Dam assumed he had come to visit her husband before he died.

And so began an unusual courtship, with Andrew visiting Mr. van Dam twice a week but spending as much time as he could with Corrie. He found her to be just as attractive as ever, with a mature faith and a peace in spite of the impending death of her father.

In late October 1957, Andrew received a visa to enter Hungary. He had applied for the visa so long ago that he had almost forgotten about it. But before he left for Hungary, he decided to ask Corrie to marry him and to let her think and pray about her answer while he was gone. However, on the day he had chosen to ask Corrie to be his wife, Corrie's father died, and Andrew got caught up helping to make the funeral arrangements.

Three weeks passed before Andrew felt that the time was again right to ask Corrie to marry him. It was not a polished proposal, and Andrew spent most of the time dwelling on the strange life Corrie would have if she married him. Despite this, Corrie promised to think about it and give him an answer when he returned from Hungary.

Never had one of his trips behind the Iron Curtain seemed so long to Andrew as he wondered what Corrie's answer would be. Getting across the Hungarian border proved to be just as exciting as getting across the Yugoslav border. Once again Andrew prayed that "seeing eyes be made blind."

This time he felt that he should take the time and eat the picnic he had with him while the Volkswagen was being searched. He opened the picnic basket and paused to pray just as two soldiers opened the car door. When the soldiers saw him bow his head to pray over his food, they slammed the door shut and ran away! Andrew ate his meal, packed up his picnic basket, and drove unchallenged across the Hungarian border. Once in the country, he headed for Budapest, the capital.

As Andrew drove around Budapest, he saw the unmistakable signs of the uprising that had occurred the year before. Bombed-out buildings and impassable streets were everywhere. Still, Andrew was able to make his way to the home of a man he knew only as Professor B. Professor B was a Christian who held a prestigious position in a large university in the city. The professor welcomed Andrew graciously and agreed to be his interpreter during the time he was in Hungary.

Andrew soon learned that following the uprising, the Hungarian government had cracked down on Christian churches. Many pastors had been dismissed from their positions and forced to have nothing more to do with their congregations. Only those pastors who were willing to compromise and adjust their message to the government's views were left alone. "Adjusting," Andrew learned, meant not only embracing the government's political point of view but also not teaching what the government considered to be religious superstitions, such as miracle stories, Creation, original sin, the fall of man, even that Jesus Christ was the Son of God.

Christians had found ways around these restrictions, however. Weddings and funerals became the place where the gospel was now preached. On a number of occasions, Andrew found himself at the wedding of people he had never met before. He would stand and congratulate the bride and groom and then preach the hardest-hitting salvation message he could. He also used the same approach he had used in Czechoslovakia, speaking in churches where he brought greetings from Christians in the West and then brought greetings from Jesus Christ, using the opportunity to preach a sermon.

Andrew was kept busy throughout his time in Hungary. It was just as well because it kept his mind off Corrie—to some degree. But finally his time in Hungary was over, and he headed back to Holland as fast as he could, eager to learn Corrie's decision.

When he reached Holland, instead of going to Sint Pancras, Andrew made his way to Haarlem, where Corrie was now working at a hospital. When Corrie got off work at eleven in the evening, Andrew was waiting outside for her.

"I'm back, Corrie," Andrew said as she emerged from the front door of the hospital. "I love you, and I'll love you whether the answer is yes or no."

"Andy, I love you too," Corrie replied. "You know I'm going to worry about you and miss you and pray for you no matter what. So I think I should be your worried wife rather than your cranky friend."

Andrew could hardly believe what he had just heard: Corrie wanted to be his wife!

The following week the two of them went to a jewelry store in Haarlem and bought wedding rings. In Holland it was the custom to wear the wedding ring on the left hand during the engagement and transfer it to the right hand during the marriage ceremony. Andrew could not have been happier as he looked at the ring on the finger of his left hand.

Several weeks after returning to Holland, Andrew received a letter from Professor B, telling him what a blessing his trip had been to the Christians in Hungary. But there was also a sad side to the letter. Professor B informed Andrew that he had lost his job at the university. He said it had nothing to do with his being Andrew's interpreter, but Andrew wasn't so sure. "Do not be sad: many have given up far more for their Savior," Professor B ended his letter.

Andrew and Corrie were married in Alkmaar on June 27, 1958, surrounded by their families, nurses from the hospital in Haarlem, workers from the chocolate factory, Uncle Hoppy from England, and friends from WEC.

Following the wedding Andrew took Corrie's hand, and looking into her eyes, he said, "Corrie, we don't know where the road leads, do we?"

"No, Andrew, we don't," Corrie replied, "but let's go there together."

Chapter 15

Nerves of Steel

After their wedding Andrew and Corrie moved into the room above the garden shed that had originally been built for Andrew's father. The room had little space: most of it was taken up with clothes—a ton of clothes. In response to the magazine articles Andrew had written about his experiences in the refugee camps, many Dutch people had bundled up clothes for the refugees at the camps in West Berlin and sent them directly to Andrew. As Andrew embarked upon married life, hundreds of parcels had begun to arrive for him. Some of the clothes they contained were dirty, and Corrie set to work washing and ironing them. Some of the clothes also contained fleas, and the van der Bijls had to get used to being attacked by the tiny black insects whenever they entered their bedroom.

Still, Andrew was grateful to have somewhere to live, though it brought the number of people in the one-bathroom van der Bijl house to eight. Andrew's brother Cornelius and his wife, along with his sister Geltje and her husband, Arie, and their two small children, lived in the house. This often led to a line to use the bathroom.

In the fall Andrew and Corrie decided it was time to deliver some of the winter clothes to the refugees in West Berlin. They loaded up the blue Volkswagen and set off for Germany. When they reached the refugee camps, conditions there were much as Andrew had expected them to be. But Corrie, even though Andrew had tried to prepare her for the squalor and hopelessness she would encounter, was still shocked by it all.

After distributing the clothes to the grateful refugees, Andrew felt that he should make a visit to see what conditions were like in Communist East Germany. Corrie decided to stay on at one of the refugee camps, where she was helping to set up health and hygiene procedures. Andrew hated to leave her behind, but he realized that his wife wanted to be where she felt she could be of the most use.

Finding Bibles and other Christian materials in German was no problem, since they were produced and sold freely in West Berlin. Andrew filled his car with the literature and headed for the Brandenburg Gate to cross into Communist East Berlin. The guards at the crossing did not seem to care what Andrew had in the car, and Andrew soon found out why. The East German government did not ban Bibles; it waged a much more insidious war against Christianity—a war of imitation.

Andrew learned that for every Christian ceremony, the East German government had created an equivalent nonreligious ceremony: East German babies were expected to be "welcomed," not baptized; "youth consecration to the state" services were held instead of the traditional Lutheran confirmation service; and even wedding and funeral ceremonies mimicked Christian ones. All of these imitation ceremonies that the government encouraged were devoid of the spiritual meaning and power of their Christian counterparts.

Church leaders in East Germany were "strongly urged" to have the members of their congregations participate in the State ceremonies and to encourage their children to be "good citizens" of East Germany. Because of this, many young people could not see much use for "old-time" religion.

Andrew decided to stir up Christians in East Germany to embark upon mission work, but even here they were discouraged. "How can we go anywhere?" they asked him. "We can't get a visa to leave the country, and there are roadblocks at every turn. We are separated from the rest of the world."

The mission workers sounded disheartened until Andrew reminded them that they had a mission field all around them. Millions of East Germans were hearing a "secular gospel" from the state, and half a million Russian soldiers were stationed throughout the country. If that was not a mission field, Andrew told them, he did not know what was. His message seemed to invigorate the church, and many new opportunities for evangelizing were discovered right at their doorsteps.

Andrew returned to West Berlin in high spirits, but his exuberance was soon dampened when he saw Corrie. Three weeks in the refugee camp had left her tired and ill. Andrew wondered whether he had done the right thing in asking his wife to share this strange lifestyle with him. One thing he knew for sure: Corrie needed a break from her work in the refugee camp. Of course she objected that there was still so much to do in the camp that she could not leave, but Andrew pressed ahead and made plans to take her with him on his next trip, this time back to Yugoslavia.

Soon Andrew and Corrie had the visas they needed, and the young couple headed for Zagreb, Yugoslavia. They had no trouble crossing the border, and Andrew noted that a husband-and-wife team aroused fewer suspicions than did a single man crossing the border.

Back in Zagreb, Andrew again met up with Nikola, and the two teamed up to preach throughout the city. Andrew was grateful that Nikola was willing to interpret for him again, since Nikola had been fined for doing it during Andrew's previous trip and told that if he spoke in a church again, he would have to withdraw from engineering school.

One week later, however, it was Andrew and Corrie who ran afoul of the authorities. While they were sitting at dinner with some other Christians, there was a knock at the door. Within seconds the police were demanding to see Andrew's and Corrie's passports and visas. Andrew soon realized that they knew who he was and where he had been, including his last trip into Yugoslavia. Although it was no use to try to cover anything up, Andrew nonetheless gave short answers to their questions. In response, the police officer in charge took out a big red stamp and stamped "No Return" across both of their visas. "You are to leave immediately," he said.

Corrie was shaken by the experience, and the following morning she and Andrew loaded up the Volkswagen and headed for the border. Andrew spent much of the trip back to West Berlin trying to calm Corrie down. "I was so scared," she kept saying. "I don't know how you do it, Andrew. You must have nerves of steel!"

Andrew smiled to himself as he thought about this. He could see how so many of the circumstances in his past had prepared him for what he was doing: the childhood espionage games he had played in the village; his experience in the Dutch Resistance during the war, stealing guns and sabotaging cars; and his time in the military, where he had to stay focused and calm under fire while people were dying around him. "Yes," Andrew told himself, "all things do work together for good for those who love God and are called according to His purposes."

When they reached West Berlin, Andrew and Corrie stopped in at the refugee camp where Corrie had been helping out. There they found a fat envelope waiting for Andrew. In it were travel documents to enter Bulgaria and Romania. Andrew was ecstatic. This meant that he could go deeper than ever behind the Iron Curtain. But first he had to get Corrie home and find out why she was feeling so ill.

The cause of Corrie's illness turned out to be the biggest surprise of all. The doctor in Sint Pancras shook his head after he examined Corrie. "There's nothing wrong with her that seven more months won't cure," he declared.

"You mean, you mean...?" Andrew stammered.

The doctor broke into a broad smile. "Yes. Congratulations. You are going to be a father in June."

Andrew was stunned. He was so happy to finally have a wife that he had not given much thought to being a father. He spent the rest of the week adjusting to the idea.

Two months rolled by, and in early 1959 Andrew was feeling restless again. He had decided to stay close to home until the baby was born, but now June seemed a long way away. A shipment of Romanian and Bulgarian Bibles had arrived for him from the British and Foreign Bible Society, and Andrew began wondering whether this was a sign that he should deliver them—soon.

Andrew discussed his thoughts with Corrie, who with morning sickness behind her was now feeling much better. Corrie was not excited about the idea, but after thinking about it, she told Andrew that in agreeing to marry him, she had also agreed to be a partner in his ministry, and if God was telling him to go, then he should go. She helped him load up the car with Bibles and camping gear. After giving his wife a final kiss good-bye, Andrew once again headed off across Europe.

The quickest way to Bulgaria from Holland was through Yugoslavia, so before setting out, Andrew had obtained a new Dutch passport and applied for another visa at the Yugoslav consulate in Holland. As he had suspected, the wheels of bureaucracy in Communist countries moved slowly, and the consulate had not yet received word that Andrew was an undesirable and should not be issued a visa. As a result, Andrew got the visa he applied for and headed for Yugoslavia. He was not listed as an undesirable at the border crossing either, and he was allowed to cross into the country. Andrew figured that it would take the Yugoslav authorities about four days to realize that he had reentered the country and track him down. By that time he intended to be in Bulgaria.

On his way through Yugoslavia, Andrew stopped off to visit Jamil and Nikola, who furnished him with the addresses of some churches in the south of the country that he should stop and speak at. Andrew did this, but it took him longer than expected, and on the fifth night he was still in Yugoslavia. He checked into a hotel for the night in a town fifty miles from the Bulgarian border, handing in his passport at the front desk, as he was obliged to do. He intended to drive to the border first thing in the morning and cross into Bulgaria. However, in the early hours of the morning he heard a knock at the door of his room. He opened the door, and there stood two men in business suits.

"Dress and follow us," one of the men demanded in German.

Andrew did as he was told, and the men led him out of the hotel and down the street to a large, stone building. In a room inside the building sat another man behind a desk.

"Why are you here?" the man asked in German, slapping Andrew's passport down on the desk. "Why did you come back? You were ordered not to do so."

The man did not wait for Andrew to reply. Instead he opened a drawer in the desk and pulled out a stamp and inkpad. He opened the passport, and with a quick flick of his wrist he stamped "No Return" three times in red over the visa.

"You will leave Yugoslavia within twenty-four hours. You will contact no one in the country, and we will phone the border guards in Trieste and advise them to expect you," the man said when he had finished stamping.

"Trieste?" Andrew said. "But I am on my way to Bulgaria. Please, may I be allowed to cross the Bulgarian border?"

"You must retrace your route north and leave at Trieste," the man snapped. "Are you clear on that?"

Andrew nodded dejectedly.

The next morning Andrew set out north toward Trieste. This was not what he had expected, and his spirits began to flag as he drove along. Now the only route open to him to get to Bulgaria was to cross into Italy and drive south all the way to Brindisi, catch a ferry to Greece, and drive north to the Bulgarian border. This would add about fifteen hundred miles to his journey.

As he drove south through Italy, Andrew began to grow depressed and frustrated. The Italian roads were clogged with traffic and people, slowing his progress. And to make matters worse, his back began to hurt more than it had ever hurt before in his life. By the time he reached Brindisi, Andrew could barely walk. Still the detour had put him on a tight schedule, and he had no time to seek medical attention.

Once in Greece, Andrew headed straight for the Bulgarian border. To his dismay, the Greek roads were potholed and in terrible condition, and once again Andrew's progress was slowed. In addition, the road signs were all in Greek, causing Andrew to get lost several times and forcing him to have to backtrack.

As he got closer to the border, Andrew stopped in the town of Serrai, where he received another blow. He was told that only diplomats were allowed to cross into Bulgaria at the border crossing he was headed for. Since there were no other border crossings into Bulgaria from Greece, Andrew was advised that if he wanted to enter the country, he would have to head east to Turkey and cross into Bulgaria from there. Andrew could scarcely believe it—Turkey was over two hundred miles from where he was. And if that were not enough, the longer he sat driving in his Volkswagen, the sorer his back got. But since he could do nothing about it, he drove east toward Turkey.

As he drove along, Andrew became more and more depressed and despondent. This was not what he had planned for his journey. His back was now so sore that he wondered whether he would even be able to walk when he got to Bulgaria. He wondered whether this was any kind of life for a husband and soon-to-be father.

Driving along, Andrew noticed a road sign in Greek, and underneath the Greek was written the name "Filippi." This was the site of ancient Philippi in the Bible. Andrew had to stop and see the place. He pulled the Volkswagen over to the side of the road and climbed out. He hobbled over to the chain-link fence that surrounded the site and looked out on the ruins of the city. This was where the apostle Paul had converted Lydia, who was considered to be the first European Christian convert. It was also the place where Paul and Silas had been imprisoned for their faith but God had miraculously set them free.

As he looked out on Philippi and thought about these events, Andrew felt his depression fall away. Faith began to rise in his heart. The same God who had guided Paul was guiding him. And if Paul could trust and praise Him from his prison cell, who was Andrew to complain about his situation? All he could do was trust that God was in control of his circumstances.

As he turned to walk back to the car, Andrew noticed something else. Not only had his faith been lifted, but also his back no longer hurt. He was walking tall and easy, with no pain.

Andrew drove on into Turkey and crossed the border into Bulgaria without incident. He then headed for the capital city of Sofia, where he made contact with a man named Petroff, whose name someone in Yugoslavia had given him.

Petroff explained to Andrew that the churches he saw with their doors open were puppet churches that were controlled by the government and denied the life-changing power of the gospel. The real Christian church had gone underground. Over the next two weeks, Andrew and Petroff visited many of these underground churches, which met secretly in people's houses and apartments.

Bibles in Bulgaria were in short supply, and at each church meeting Andrew attended, he took one of the Bulgarian Bibles and presented it to the group. The members of the church would gasp when they saw it, and as they passed it from one to the other to examine it, tears would run down their cheeks.

Finally it was time for Andrew to move on to Romania. But as he was about to drive north to the Danube River, which marked the border with Romania, a group of people came to Andrew and begged him not to leave but to come and speak at their church. Andrew wished that he could, but he had to cross into Romania by the date on his visa, and that date was now only a day away.

At the Romanian border Andrew watched in shock as the three cars in line in front of him were almost torn apart as the guards searched them. He knew that if his car was subjected to the same level of search, the guards would easily find the Romanian Bibles he was carrying. As he prayed about what to do, Andrew felt that he should be open about what he was carrying into the country. He reached into the backseat of the Volkswagen and pulled out several of the Bibles he had hidden there. He piled them beside him on the front seat, where the border guards would be sure to see them.

Finally it was his turn. Andrew drove the car forward and stopped in front of the barrier. He rolled down the window and handed his passport to the guard. His heart pounded as the guard looked at the passport and then wrote something down on a piece of paper. Finally the guard looked inside the car, right where the Bibles were stacked on the front seat. Then, much to Andrew's surprise and relief, the guard handed back the passport and waved him on into Romania.

Andrew had expected Romania to be much like Bulgaria, but as he drove along, he saw how mistaken he was. Romania was the strictest police state he had visited so far. Police roadblocks were situated throughout the country to check people's papers, and unlike the Bulgarians, whom Andrew had found to be warm and friendly, the Romanians were deeply fearful and suspicious of each other and especially of foreigners like him.

Because of the people's fear and suspicion, it took Andrew a while before he found a Christian willing to talk to him and interpret for him. As he talked, he learned that the way the Romanian government controlled the church was through a program of consolidation. The government would consolidate the churches in several villages down to a single congregation, and the empty church buildings would be confiscated. The effect of this consolidation was to cripple the church. Now, instead of attending their local church, people would have to travel to the next village or the village beyond that to attend services. This inconvenience caused many people to stop attending church after a consolidation had taken place.

Andrew left the Romanian Bibles he had carried into the country with his contact, who would know how and where to distribute the Bibles so that they were of the most use to the greatest number of Christians.

Finally it was time for Andrew to retrace his route and head back to Holland. Because of the delay in getting to Bulgaria, he was departing for home later than he had planned. Andrew sped along as fast as the road conditions and the Volkswagen would allow. It was now late May, and Corrie was due to give birth any day now.

Relief flooded through Andrew when he finally drove across the border into Holland. It felt wonderful to be home again, and he was hopeful that he was not too late for the birth of the baby.

Chapter 16

Into the Soviet Union

Much to his relief, Andrew found that Corrie had not yet given birth by the time he arrived home. A week later, on June 4, 1959, Corrie delivered a baby boy, whom they named Joppie. Three weeks after the baby's birth, Andrew and Corrie celebrated their first wedding anniversary.

At the same time, Andrew's sister Geltje was expecting her third child, and his brother Cornelius's wife was expecting her first. Counting the new babies, six adults and five children would soon be living in the old van der Bijl house. Andrew could see that there were just too many people for the house, and he knew that it was time for him and Corrie to find somewhere else to live. But where could they go? At the time, housing was scarce in

Holland, and even if they could find a place, they had very little money to pay for it. Small amounts of money dribbled in from people as a result of the magazine articles Andrew continued to write and publish about the plight of Christians behind the Iron Curtain. Andrew also received offerings from the various churches where he spoke, but he and Corrie had no savings for a house. Even the clothes they and Joppie wore came from the donation boxes.

Andrew and Corrie could see no way through their situation except to pray. Within weeks a house in the village came up for sale, and the owner offered to sell it to Andrew for half its value. This was a generous offer, but coming up with enough money to cover half or even a quarter of its value was still a distant dream.

Andrew decided to call Mr. Whetstra and discuss the situation with him. Mr. Whetstra offered to buy the house and allow Andrew to pay him back when he could. This was a startling offer, and a humbling one. Andrew and Corrie discussed it together and finally agreed to accept Mr. Whetstra's offer. They moved into their new home when Joppie was three months old. Six months after moving in, they learned that Corrie was expecting another baby!

Baby Mark was born in 1960. That same year Andrew made his first trip to the Soviet Union. As he had in 1955, when he went to Warsaw, he traveled with a group of young people from Holland, Germany, and Denmark who were going to attend a youth festival in Moscow. He was in the country for only two weeks, but in that time he learned a lot about the plight of Christians in the Soviet Union. As with the authorities in Romania, the Soviet government was attempting to control the church through a program of consolidation, so much so that only one Protestant church was now left open in the city. And the next open Protestant church was one hundred miles away in a town outside Moscow.

While in Moscow Andrew attended the open Protestant church, and he was surprised by what he saw. The old church was built to hold one thousand people, but on the Sunday morning he attended, two thousand people were packed into the place. People were sitting two to a seat, while others stood in the center aisle and along the sides of the church. The place was so packed that when the collection was taken up, people had to pass their banknotes overhead to the front. And they wrote their prayer requests on pieces of paper that they then turned into paper darts and aimed at the front of the church.

At the end of his trip to the Soviet Union, Andrew determined that in the not too distant future he would make a return visit there, this time by car so that he could carry Russian Bibles into the country.

The following year, in 1961, Corrie gave birth to a third son, whom they named Paul. Andrew now had a wife, three children, and a unique ministry to support. Everywhere he went, Andrew saw so much need that a question began to form in his mind: should he continue to work alone, or was it time to invite other "smugglers" to join him in his ministry?

This was not an easy question to answer. Corrie was all for the idea of spreading the ministry load, but Andrew was concerned that the operation would become more vulnerable if he recruited novices to join him. But as he prayed about the situation, one name came to his mind—Hans Gruber.

Hans was a six-foot seven-inch tall Dutchman whom Andrew had met in one of the refugee camps in Austria. He was built like an ox, and there was no way he could disappear into a crowd. He was also one of the clumsiest people Andrew had ever met. But none of these things mattered once Andrew heard Hans preach in the refugee camp. When Hans spoke, everyone listened. Even the incorrigible teenage boys would stand out in the pouring rain listening to him.

Andrew decided to write to Hans and ask him to join him on a trip to the Soviet Union. The letter Andrew received back gave him goose bumps. Hans confided that he had always felt that one day he would work in the Soviet Union. In fact, he reported that when he was in the sixth grade, while he was looking at a map of Russia, he heard a voice in his head saying, "Someday you will work for Me in that land."

Andrew was even more encouraged to learn that Hans had done whatever he could to prepare for this calling. Hans had learned Russian and was ready to drop everything at a moment's notice and travel with Andrew.

After exchanging several more letters, everything was arranged, including a new car for the venture.

The blue Volkswagen had been driven over two hundred thousand kilometers by now, and it was no longer reliable enough to make another long trip—assuming that Hans could even cram his six-foot seven-inch frame into the tiny vehicle. Money arrived just at the right moment, and Andrew was able to purchase a new Opel station wagon to replace the Volkswagen. The new vehicle was big enough to sleep in the back of, and hundreds more Bibles could be transported in it. The only problem was that Hans could not drive, but Andrew was confident that he would learn along the way.

Andrew and Hans set off for the Soviet Union, crossing Holland, Germany, and Poland to get there. Two thousand miles later, they were in Moscow, driving along the edge of Red Square, past the mausoleum where Lenin was entombed, on their way to the campsite they had registered to stay at. They arrived at the campsite on a Thursday afternoon. After Andrew and Hans had settled in, they set out on foot to find the Protestant church that Andrew had attended two years before. Back then there had been a Thursday night meeting. Sure enough, Andrew and Hans arrived at the church just as the service was beginning.

Andrew did not recognize anyone in the congregation. He began praying that God would show him the right person to contact about distributing the Russian Bibles he had brought into the country. As soon as the meeting was over, his attention was drawn to an elderly, bald man standing alone. Andrew felt the now familiar voice inside telling him that this man was his contact. He was not surprised when Hans sidled up to him and said quietly in Dutch, "I've spotted our man. He's the bald man standing over there."

Andrew smiled to himself. How good it was to have a partner.

The two of them walked over to the man, and Hans introduced them in Russian.

The man frowned. "You speak German?" he asked.

Hans nodded. "German and Dutch. We are Dutchmen," he replied.

The man burst into a grin. "I am German! My grandparents moved to Siberia from Germany, and we still speak German in our home," he said.

"You live in Siberia?" Andrew interjected.

"Yes," the man replied, looking around. "I am part of a small church there. There are one hundred and fifty in the congregation, and not one Bible among us. One day God gave me a dream, and in that dream I went to Moscow and someone gave me a Bible for our church. Moscow is two thousand miles from my home. At first I would not consider going, but the dream was very alive to me, and eventually I could not resist, so I came. And that is why I am here. But where would I find a Bible in this city...?" his voice trailed off.

Andrew's heart beat fast as he shot Hans a glance. This was far too amazing to be coincidence! Hans reached under his coat, pulled out a big Russian Bible, and handed it to the man. The man took it and held it out, staring at it. Then, like a floodgate opening, he babbled his thanks while he hugged Hans and Andrew.

Andrew tried to calm the man down before he drew too much attention to them all. "We'll meet you here tomorrow morning at ten," he whispered. "We have four more Bibles for you."

"How much do they cost?" the man asked.

"They are a gift from the church in the West to strengthen and encourage you," Andrew replied.

The man slipped the Bible under his coat, wiped his eyes, and nodded. "Tomorrow at ten," he said. "I will be here."

The following morning at ten o'clock, Andrew and Hans walked into the empty sanctuary and sat down in a pew at the back. The minutes ticked by. It was ten thirty, and still the man from Siberia had not arrived. At ten forty-five Andrew heard footsteps enter the sanctuary. He turned, expecting to see the man from Siberia. Instead it was the pastor of the church whom Andrew had met and talked with on his first visit to the church two years before.

"Hello. Are you waiting for someone?" the pastor asked.

"Yes, someone we met last night," Andrew replied.

"I'm afraid your Siberian friend won't be coming," the pastor said.

Andrew and Hans stared questioningly at the pastor.

"At each service there are members of the secret police in attendance. They saw you and the man talking, and now the secret police have 'spoken' to him, and so he will not be coming to meet you. But you have something for him?" the pastor asked.

Andrew looked at Hans and knew that they were both thinking the same thing: could they trust the pastor? Finally they decided they could, and they gave almost imperceptible nods to each other. Then Hans opened the bag they had with them and pulled out the four Russian Bibles.

As the pastor reached out to take the Bibles, Andrew said, "These aren't the only Bibles we have with us."

The pastor raised his eyebrows. "How many Bibles do you have?" he asked.

"Over one hundred. They are hidden in our car," Andrew replied.

"Over one hundred!" the pastor said incredulously. "I cannot deal with that many Bibles. It is not a crime to own a Bible in Russia, but it is a crime to distribute them. I have already been imprisoned and cruelly treated for my faith once, and I cannot face that again," he said, staring at the scars on his fingers and hands.

"I understand your situation," Andrew said. "Is there someone else who might be willing to help us?"

"Markov," the pastor replied. "Be in front of the GUM department store in your car at one this afternoon, and I will arrange for Markov to meet you there. But be careful."

At one o'clock that afternoon, Andrew and Hans sat in the Opel station wagon outside the store. Several minutes after one, a man got out of a car parked about one hundred yards away. He walked past the Opel, staring in through the windshield at Andrew and Hans. Then he turned and walked back. This time he stopped by the station wagon and said, "Brother Andrew?"

"Are you Markov?" Andrew asked.

The man nodded.

"Then greetings in the Name of the Lord," Andrew said.

"We are going to do something bold," Markov explained. "We are going to exchange the Bibles from your car to mine within two minutes of Red Square."

Andrew and Hans looked surprised.

"Do not worry. No one will ever suspect what we are doing in such a location," Markov said, trying to soothe their fears.

Andrew and Hans followed Markov past Red Square, and then they turned in to a street with a wall down one side and apartments on the other side. Andrew parked the Opel behind Markov's car and got out while Hans sat inside praying. Andrew and Markov quickly shuffled the cartons of Bibles from one car to the other.

When they were done, Markov gave Andrew a handshake. "By next week these Bibles will be in the hands of pastors all over Russia," he said before getting into his car and driving off.

With their mission of delivering the Russian Bibles complete, Andrew and Hans made their way home through the Ukraine, since they had a carton of Ukrainian Bibles with them and wanted to distribute them. In the Ukraine they stopped at various Christian meetings along the way, encouraging believers wherever they could. In one village Andrew was fascinated to see a pocket-sized Ukrainian Bible. All the Russian and Ukrainian Bibles Andrew had seen before tended to be big and bulky, so he was amazed to see such a small one. As he held it in his hand, possibilities opened up to Andrew. Why not print small copies of the Bible in the various languages of Eastern Europe? That way he could load two, three, or even four times as many Bibles into the station wagon and deliver them behind the Iron Curtain. The owner of the pocket-sized Bible gave his Bible to Andrew so that he could take it back to Holland and show the printers there just how small a Bible could be printed on fine onionskin paper.

Just before they crossed into Hungary, Andrew and Hans stopped at a Ukrainian Baptist church, where Andrew saw something he never seen before—a pastor preaching a sermon without a Bible. After the service the two men introduced themselves to the pastor and began talking about theological issues. When the pastor cited a Bible reference, Andrew followed along in his own Dutch Bible so that he could understand exactly what was being said. But as they talked, Andrew noticed that the pastor was paying more and more attention to the Dutch Bible than he was to the conversation. Eventually the pastor blurted out, "Brother Andrew, I have no Bible."

Andrew's heart dropped. They did not have a single Ukrainian Bible left to give him. Or did they? With a surge of joy Andrew remembered the pocket-sized Bible he was keeping as a sample. How could he justify keeping it when there was a pastor who preached to thousands without a Bible? Andrew leapt up, ran outside, and retrieved the tiny Bible from under the car seat. He returned and handed it to the pastor. "This is for you to keep," he said.

The pastor could not at first grasp the idea of owning his own Bible. Then he pulled the Bible to his chest, and tears rolled down his cheeks. Andrew knew that he had done the right thing in giving away the tiny Bible.

During the journey homeward, Andrew replayed the scene over and over again in his mind. He was consumed with the idea of printing small Bibles in the Slavic languages. The only thing holding him back was the cost of such a venture. He and Corrie already had enough financial stress, raising three small boys and supporting the ministry.

Chapter 17

The Bamboo Curtain

Back in Holland Andrew was consumed with the need to print small Bibles in the languages of Eastern Europe. He got quotes from various printers for producing the Bibles, and the best price he could find was three dollars per Bible, provided that he print five thousand copies at a time. This meant that Andrew needed to come up with fifteen thousand dollars. Andrew prayed about the need and asked God to provide the money, but no large sums were donated for the project.

Unwilling to give up on the idea, Andrew and Corrie agreed that they should put their house on the market and use the money they received from the sale of the house to pay for the printing of the Bibles. Corrie was expecting a fourth child, but when she and Andrew weighed the need for Bibles behind the Iron Curtain against their own family needs, they decided they could not keep the house.

Strangely enough, even though there was a housing shortage in Holland, the house did not sell immediately. And while Andrew and Corrie waited for it to sell, the Dutch Bible Society agreed to fund the project, with Andrew paying them back half the cost when he could. Andrew and Corrie were relieved that they would not have to sell the house after all. Soon afterward, their first daughter, whom they named Stephanie, was born.

One day in 1965, as Andrew was speaking in a Dutch church, a man came up to him, speaking English with an American accent. "Brother Andrew, you have so much to share with us in the United States. Have you ever spoken there?"

Andrew shook his head. He had been invited to speak in the United States on several occasions, but he had turned down the invitations, not wanting to leave the impression that he was on a speaking tour just to raise funds from a rich nation.

"You should come. The people in America need to know what is going on in Eastern Europe. They don't understand the real threat of Communism to us all," the man said.

For the first time Andrew felt that God wanted him to cross the Atlantic Ocean to America. He allowed the man, who said he was a seminary student, to plan an itinerary for him. Soon everything was planned, and Andrew was on his way to the United States.

When Andrew arrived in the country, a rude shock awaited him. The man who had sponsored the trip belonged to a militant anti-Communist group that believed that killing Communists was the best way to free the world. The members of the group carried rifles with them everywhere, even to class! The group wanted Andrew to preach a message of hate and revenge, but Andrew wanted to preach about love and positive action. Not surprisingly, the sponsor withdrew his support, and Andrew found himself broke and stranded in the United States.

Andrew wired Corrie to send him some money so that he could get home. While he waited for the money to arrive, he was asked to preach at a large church in Los Angeles. Andrew was disappointed that this one speaking engagement was not going to bring the level of awareness to his cause that he had hoped, but he figured that one speaking engagement in the United States was better than none.

Following the service, a tall, slim man introduced himself. His name was John Sherrill, and he was an editor of the well-known Christian magazine *Guideposts.*

"Would you like to have breakfast with me tomorrow?" John asked. "I really think you have a story that North Americans need to hear."

At the meeting the following morning, Andrew spent two hours telling John his story. When Andrew had finished, John was even more convinced that he had to write an article about Brother Andrew and his work. In the course of the next two days, Andrew provided John with the information he needed, and then he flew on to Hong Kong.

While in Hong Kong, Andrew decided that he should try to salvage something good from the trip. He applied for a visa to enter Communist China to see what was left of the church there.

China differed from the Communist countries of Eastern Europe in two important ways. It had been under Communist control for only sixteen years, since 1949, and Western missionaries had been working in China for only a little over one hundred years when the Communists expelled them. As a result, only a small percentage of the population had ever been Christians.

Local contacts in Hong Kong told Andrew that it was impossible to get a visa to enter China, especially since he had an entry stamp for the United States in his passport. But much to everyone's surprise, Andrew was granted the visa he requested. Quickly he gathered up a number of copies of the Bible in Chinese to take behind the Bamboo Curtain, Asia's equivalent of the Iron Curtain.

At the border a Chinese guard unzipped Andrew's bag and looked inside, right at the Mandarin Bibles. Andrew waited to see what would happen. Would he be arrested? Or would the Bibles be seized? To Andrew's surprise the guard did nothing. Instead he asked, "Do you have a camera?"

"No," Andrew replied.

With that the guard waved him on into China.

While it had been easy to get the Bibles across the border into China, Andrew soon found that distributing them was a different matter. In the years since the Communists had taken over China, they had not only expelled all the foreign missionaries but also succeeded in almost totally destroying the Christian church. They had replaced the Christian church with a state-sanctioned church called the Three-Self Patriotic Movement. Every pastor and member of this church had to be registered with the state. Pastors also were forbidden to evangelize or teach religion to children, and they were not to preach on tithing, keeping Sunday as a day of rest, healing, and the Second Coming of Christ. As a result, the church was small and powerless.

As he made his way back to Holland, Andrew thought about his experience in China. There was enough work there to keep one hundred workers—or more like a thousand—busy behind the Bamboo Curtain. On top of that, Andrew dreamed of visiting every Communist country in Eastern Europe once a year. The sheer enormity of the task was overwhelming, and Andrew knew that he would have to recruit more workers.

When he was out speaking, people would often ask Andrew if they could join his ministry. He always gave them the same answer: "Make a trip or two behind the Iron Curtain on your own, see if you are a good fit for what we do, and then come back and talk to me." This was the only way of recruiting that he thought was a fair test of a person's commitment.

The only problem was that no one had ever actually done what he suggested—that is, until he got home and found a young Dutchman named Marcus waiting for him.

"I've been to Yugoslavia like you said, and I passed out tracts there. Now here I am, sir, reporting for my next assignment," Marcus said.

Andrew was delighted. Right when he felt that the work needed to grow, God had sent him a determined worker. Andrew put Marcus to work right away, smuggling Bibles into Yugoslavia and Bulgaria.

Meanwhile Andrew planned a trip for himself and Hans Gruber into another Communist country—Cuba. They left for Cuba late in 1965, having been able to get visas to enter the country because they were Dutch citizens and not Americans.

In Cuba Andrew found no shortage of Bibles as he had in other Communist countries, and he was able to speak reasonably freely in churches. However, the church was under attack by Communist dictator Fidel Castro. Pastors had been classified as "nonproductive." As a result, they were not issued coupons that allowed them to buy food or clothing. And because they were classified as nonproductive, many pastors were rounded up and forced to work on labor gangs, often in the sugarcane fields. In this way the Cuban government believed that over time the Christian church in the country would wither and die. Despite this pressure from the government, Andrew encountered a great deal of spiritual hunger among the people of Cuba.

On his way back to Holland, Andrew stopped off in the United States, where he visited John Sherrill. John had news for Andrew. The article he had written for *Guideposts* magazine had produced a tremendous response, and people wanted to know more about Andrew's experiences in Communist countries. Because of this, John and his wife, Elizabeth, wanted to write a full-length book on Andrew's life and experiences.

Andrew did not quite know what to do. Publishing a book would mean a lot of exposure for his ministry, which he hoped would lead to more prayer and financial support and possibly more workers. But, and it was a huge *but,* through the book, Communist governments could also learn of his work and ban him from ever entering their countries again.

It was a difficult decision, but as he prayed about it, Andrew felt that the Sherrills should go ahead and write the book. He asked them to do all they could to disguise his identity, referring to him only as Brother Andrew and changing some names, including the name of Sint Pancras to Witte, in the book. Even so, Andrew knew that anyone who really wanted to find out who he was would not have much difficulty doing so.

A year later, in 1966, China was in the headlines day after day. Mao Tse-tung, China's Communist leader, led his Red Guards into what was being called a Cultural Revolution. Anyone who had an education or enjoyed reading or learning about the outside world was targeted, and many thousands of people were killed or arrested. From the information Andrew was able to gather, the Cultural Revolution was decimating the few Christian churches still active in China. Andrew's heart ached for the Christians in China, and he prayed fervently for funds to help the situation there.

The answer to his prayers came in the form of royalties from the Sherrills' book, *God's Smuggler,* published the following year. The book about Andrew's life and ministry was an instant bestseller. For the first time Andrew had enough money to outfit a fleet of cars, hire a mechanic to keep them all in top working order, and print the small Bibles he needed to take into Communist countries.

As his organization in Holland grew, Andrew did not forget about China. He decided that something had to be done there—something big! Andrew soon learned about an American ex-marine living in the Philippines. The man worked for a Christian radio station that broadcast into China in the Mandarin language. The man went by the name Brother David, and he was passionate about finding a way to get Bibles into China. He had even compiled a list of Chinese Christians who were ready to receive and distribute them.

Andrew felt sure that he would join forces with Brother David before too long. In the meantime he kept busy seeking out Christians who were being persecuted or suppressed. He spent time in Vietnam raising awareness of the plight of the war orphans and traveled to Africa to see for himself how Communists were infiltrating the governments of countries there.

The ministry organization kept growing. As well as having an office in Holland, Andrew had opened offices in the United States, England, and Asia. With four offices, the time seemed right to give the ministry an official name. Andrew chose "Open Doors with Brother Andrew." Open doors referred to a verse in Revelation 3:8 that says, "I have set before you an open door, which no one is able to shut."

In September 1975 Andrew decided to convene a conference in Manila, the Philippines. The event was dubbed the "Love China" conference, and its purpose was to express the love of Christians for the people of China. Hundreds of delegates from fifty-five different mission organizations and twenty-three countries attended the conference. A number of speakers educated the attendees on the political and social situation in China. Andrew then challenged those at the conference to focus on the plight of the suffering Christians in China by going there and encouraging them and taking them Bibles, as well as evangelizing among the Chinese people. Andrew grew frustrated when some of the attendees told him that what he suggested was not practical, that the door to China was "closed."

Brother David was at the conference, and he and Andrew spent much time together talking, planning, and praying. They were both determined to join forces and do more to help the suffering Chinese church.

Chapter 18

The Fight Continues

When Andrew made his first trip into China, he had been discouraged at the state of the officially sanctioned churches he saw and by the fact that the results of the expelled foreign missionaries' work seemed to have evaporated in the face of persecution. But through his friendship with Brother David, Andrew came to see that his assessment of the situation in China had been wrong. Brother David had made numerous trips into China, and he reported that there were two types of churches operating in China: the officially sanctioned churches and also the house churches. Like the underground churches Andrew had encountered in some of the Communist countries of Eastern Europe, these latter churches met clandestinely in people's houses and apartments. According to Brother David, the work of the missionaries in China had not withered but had taken root in these churches. He estimated that millions of Chinese Christians were attending house churches across the country.

One of the great needs of these house churches, Andrew learned, was Bibles. Often they were in such short supply that a Bible would be cut apart and sections of it handed around so that people could memorize it. Workers from Open Doors soon began smuggling Bibles into China and distributing them to the house churches, but the need always vastly outstripped the supply. Then one day Andrew and Brother David came up with a bold plan to help the supply side of the equation—Project Pearl.

Project Pearl, which was named for the pearl of great price spoken of by Jesus in Matthew 13, was a plan to smuggle one million Bibles into China in one shipment. This undertaking was massive both financially and logistically. The plan was to carry the Bibles by sea to a deserted beach near Swatow, about one hundred miles north of Hong Kong. From the beach, Chinese contacts would store and then distribute the Bibles to house churches throughout the country. Andrew was kept busy raising money to pay for the project, which would cost over seven million dollars, while Brother David and other Open Doors workers planned the logistics of the delivery.

A tugboat and a barge were purchased for the project. The tugboat was named *Michael,* and the barge, *Gabriella,* after the two archangels. The Bibles, packed into 232 one-ton, watertight packages, were loaded onto the barge. Each package was roped to the next one. The plan was to float the packages ashore from the barge, using the rope to haul them ashore onto the beach.

On the night of June 18, 1981, Operation Pearl got under way. Andrew was excited when word reached him that the operation had worked almost flawlessly. Under the cover of dark, at high tide off Swatow, the 232 packages of Bibles were dumped into the water. Two small boats then pulled the packages connected by the rope to shore, where two thousand Chinese Christians were waiting to haul the Bibles in and carry them away. When almost all the Bibles had been pulled ashore, a group of soldiers on patrol happened along. The soldiers seized the remaining Bibles and tossed them back into the ocean. In all, it was estimated that about ten thousand Bibles, one percent of the total delivery, were thrown into the ocean by the soldiers. But Andrew was cheered to hear that the next day, all over Swatow, thousands of copies of black-covered Bibles were seen drying in the sun on the roofs of houses. Andrew was even more delighted with the operation when word reached him several weeks later that all of the Bibles had been successfully delivered to house churches, some of which were thousands of miles away from the beach where the Bibles had been dropped off.

By this time, many of the Communist countries of Eastern Europe were beginning to allow more Christian freedoms. Yugoslavia now let Bibles enter the country legally, and in East Germany Andrew was allowed to preach to crowds of up to four thousand people.

By 1985 the Communist countries of Eastern Europe were becoming more open toward religious freedom. Much of this came about because of the efforts of Mikhail Gorbachev, the new leader of the Soviet Union. Gorbachev instituted a series of reforms known as *glasnost* (openness) and *perestroika* (restructuring) that sought to undo seventy years of economic stagnation and political repression. Despite this growing openness, Andrew was still surprised when in 1988 Gorbachev allowed Open Doors to donate one million Russian Bibles in celebration of the one thousandth anniversary of the Russian Orthodox Church. The church then distributed the Bibles throughout the country.

This new openness continued to gain momentum, and in November 1989, the Berlin Wall, which had divided East and West Berlin since 1961, was torn down. Now Germans from both sides of the wall could have fellowship together and share their faith freely. The events were astonishing to just about everyone except Brother Andrew, who had prayed and believed for many years that Germany would one day be reunited.

In 1991 Andrew traveled to Albania, the country he had previously found to be the most repressive of all the Communist countries in Eastern Europe. While there he was allowed total freedom, and he preached to crowds totaling eight thousand people and openly distributed tens of thousands of copies of the Gospel of John and seven thousand New Testaments.

That year he also met with twelve Iranian pastors and their wives to find out how best to serve the Iranian Christians living under the grip of a fundamentalist Muslim government. Not long after the meeting, two of the pastors were imprisoned. They were subsequently releases from jail and then mysteriously murdered. Andrew was saddened by the news, but he encouraged Christians everywhere to continue reaching out to Muslims. "We are not fighting the Muslims or the Communists; we are fighting the devil," he reminded people wherever he went.

But Brother Andrew's time of fighting at the helm of Open Doors was coming to an end. In 1995, at the age of sixty-seven, he decided to step down from the role of president. His younger colleague and fellow Dutchman, Johan Campanjen, took his place, reaffirming the three aims Brother Andrew had established for the organization: (1) to deliver Bibles by whatever means possible into countries where they have been banded or restricted, (2) to train church leaders living in countries opposed to the gospel, and (3) to support and encourage individual leaders suffering for their faith.

Andrew, of course, continued to follow his life's calling; he'd never needed a title to do that. He and Corrie kept up contact with the tightly knit group of 350 workers who staffed the major offices of Open

Doors around the world. Freed from his administrative duties, Brother Andrew felt particularly drawn to strengthen the Christian church in the Middle East. In the following years he visited many Arab and Lebanese pastors. He urged them not to flee when persecuted, but to stand firm and strengthen what remains. It was the same message he had received so many years before in Warsaw, Poland.

In his travels Andrew met with many leaders in the region, among them Ahmed Yassin, the controversial leader of Hamas, a militant Islamist and Palestinian nationalist organization in the Gaza Strip, and Yasser Arafat, chairman of the Palestine Liberation Organization (PLO). Always when he met such people, Brother Andrew listened carefully to what they said and advocated for religious freedom for Christians. He was grateful when Yasser Arafat gave him permission to open a Christian bookstore in the Gaza Strip.

In 2004, Brother Andrew, along with Al Janssen, chairman of the Open Doors board of directors, co-wrote Light Force. This book profiled many courageous Christians and their communities in the Middle East that Andrew and Al had spent time with during their travels. Three years later, the duo published another book, Secret Believers: What Happens When Muslims Believe in Christ. This volume contained fictionized accounts of the many struggles Christian believers have in dealing with their families and communities in the Islamic world.

Soon after the release of Secret Believers, Andrew

turned eighty years old. By now he was starting to slow down and began spending more time in his garden growing vegetables and tending his flowers. He kept in daily contact with friends around the world and advised Christian leaders on how to deal with many difficult issues.

On January 23, 2018, Brother Andrew's wife Corrie died. They were six months short of celebrating their sixtieth wedding anniversary together. Andrew was grateful for the way Corrie had stood beside him in the many trials they'd been through as a couple.

Following his wife's death, Andrews own health began to decline. He died four years later, on September 27, 2022, at age ninety-four. His funeral was private with less than one hundred family members and invited friends in attendance. The pastor conducting the service told mourners how he once asked Brother Andrew if he had his life to live over would he do anything differently. Andrew van der Bijl, he related, nodded and in reply said he would be more radical—step out in faith more, speak up louder, love the outcast and the enemy without counting the cost. To him such actions were the mark of a man or woman who had truly encountered Christ.

Bibliography

Brother Andrew, with Dan Wooding. *Brother Andrew*. Minneapolis, Minn.: Bethany House Publishers, 1983.

Brother Andrew, with Verne Becker. *The Calling*. Nashville, Tenn.: Moorings, 1996.

Brother Andrew, with John and Elizabeth Sherrill. *God's Smuggler*. Grand Rapids, Mich.: Chosen Books, 2001.

Grady, J. Lee. "Secret Agent Man," *Charisma*, March 2005.

Millwright, Alan. *Brother Andrew: God's Undercover Agent*. Uhrichsville, Ohio: Barbour Publishing, 1999.

About the Authors

Janet and Geoff Benge are a husband and wife writing team with more than thirty years of writing experience. Janet is a former elementary school teacher. Geoff holds a degree in history. Originally from New Zealand, the Benges spent ten years serving with Youth With A Mission. They have two daughters, Laura and Shannon, and an adopted son, Lito. They make their home in the Orlando, Florida, area.

Christian Heroes: Then & Now are available in paperback, e-book, and audiobook formats, with more coming soon!

www.HeroesThenAndNow.com

Also from Janet and Geoff Benge...

More adventure-filled biographies for ages 10 to 100!

Christian Heroes: Then and Now

Gladys Aylward: The Adventure of a Lifetime • 978-1-57658-019-6
Nate Saint: On a Wing and a Prayer • 978-1-57658-017-2
Hudson Taylor: Deep in the Heart of China • 978-1-57658-016-5
Amy Carmichael: Rescuer of Precious Gems • 978-1-57658-018-9
Eric Liddell: Something Greater Than Gold • 978-1-57658-137-7
Corrie ten Boom: Keeper of the Angels' Den • 978-1-57658-136-0
William Carey: Obliged to Go • 978-1-57658-147-6
George Müller: Guardian of Bristol's Orphans • 978-1-57658-145-2
Jim Elliot: One Great Purpose • 978-1-57658-146-9
Mary Slessor: Forward into Calabar • 978-1-57658-148-3
David Livingstone: Africa's Trailblazer • 978-1-57658-153-7
Betty Greene: Wings to Serve • 978-1-57658-152-0
Adoniram Judson: Bound for Burma • 978-1-57658-161-2
Cameron Townsend: Good News in Every Language • 978-1-57658-164-3
Jonathan Goforth: An Open Door in China • 978-1-57658-174-2
Lottie Moon: Giving Her All for China • 978-1-57658-188-9
John Williams: Messenger of Peace • 978-1-57658-256-5
William Booth: Soup, Soap, and Salvation • 978-1-57658-258-9
Rowland Bingham: Into Africa's Interior • 978-1-57658-282-4
Ida Scudder: Healing Bodies, Touching Hearts • 978-1-57658-285-5
Wilfred Grenfell: Fisher of Men • 978-1-57658-292-3
Lillian Trasher: The Greatest Wonder in Egypt • 978-1-57658-305-0
Loren Cunningham: Into All the World • 978-1-57658-199-5
Florence Young: Mission Accomplished • 978-1-57658-313-5
Sundar Singh: Footprints Over the Mountains • 978-1-57658-318-0
C.T. Studd: No Retreat • 978-1-57658-288-6
Rachel Saint: A Star in the Jungle • 978-1-57658-337-1
Brother Andrew: God's Secret Agent • 978-1-57658-355-5
Clarence Jones: Mr. Radio • 978-1-57658-343-2
Count Zinzendorf: Firstfruit • 978-1-57658-262-6
John Wesley: The World His Parish • 978-1-57658-382-1
C. S. Lewis: Master Storyteller • 978-1-57658-385-2
David Bussau: Facing the World Head-on • 978-1-57658-415-6
Jacob DeShazer: Forgive Your Enemies • 978-1-57658-475-0
Isobel Kuhn: On the Roof of the World • 978-1-57658-497-2
Elisabeth Elliot: Joyful Surrender • 978-1-57658-513-9
D. L. Moody: Bringing Souls to Christ • 978-1-57658-552-8
Paul Brand: Helping Hands • 978-1-57658-536-8
Dietrich Bonhoeffer: In the Midst of Wickedness • 978-1-57658-713-3
Francis Asbury: Circuit Rider • 978-1-57658-737-9
Samuel Zwemer: The Burden of Arabia • 978-1-57658-738-6

Klaus-Dieter John: Hope in the Land of the Incas • 978-1-57658-826-2
Mildred Cable: Through the Jade Gate • 978-1-57658-886-4
John Flynn: Into the Never Never • 978-1-57658-898-7
Richard Wurmbrand: Love Your Enemies • 978-1-57658-987-8
Charles Mulli: We Are Family • 978-1-57658-894-9
John Newton: Change of Heart • 978-1-57658-909-0
Helen Roseveare: Mama Luka • 978-1-57658-910-6
Norman Grubb: Mission Builder • 978-1-57658-915-1
Albert Schweitzer • 978-1-57658-961-8

Heroes of History

George Washington Carver: From Slave to Scientist • 978-1-883002-78-7
Abraham Lincoln: A New Birth of Freedom • 978-1-883002-79-4
Meriwether Lewis: Off the Edge of the Map • 978-1-883002-80-0
George Washington: True Patriot • 978-1-883002-81-7
William Penn: Liberty and Justice for All • 978-1-883002-82-4
Harriet Tubman: Freedombound • 978-1-883002-90-9
John Adams: Independence Forever • 978-1-883002-50-3
Clara Barton: Courage under Fire • 978-1-883002-51-0
Daniel Boone: Frontiersman • 978-1-932096-09-5
Theodore Roosevelt: An American Original • 978-1-932096-10-1
Douglas MacArthur: What Greater Honor • 978-1-932096-15-6
Benjamin Franklin: Live Wire • 978-1-932096-14-9
Christopher Columbus: Across the Ocean Sea • 978-1-932096-23-1
Laura Ingalls Wilder: A Storybook Life • 978-1-932096-32-3
Orville Wright: The Flyer • 978-1-932096-34-7
Captain John Smith: A Foothold in the New World • 978-1-932096-36-1
Thomas Edison: Inspiration and Hard Work • 978-1-932096-37-8
Alan Shepard: Higher and Faster • 978-1-932096-41-5
Ronald Reagan: Destiny at His Side • 978-1-932096-65-1
Davy Crockett: Ever Westward • 978-1-932096-67-5
Milton Hershey: More Than Chocolate • 978-1-932096-82-8
Billy Graham: America's Pastor • 978-1-62486-024-9
Ben Carson: A Chance at Life • 978-1-62486-034-8
Louis Zamperini: Redemption • 978-1-62486-049-2
Elizabeth Fry: Angel of Newgate • 978-1-62486-064-5
William Wilberforce: Take Up the Fight • 978-1-62486-057-7
William Bradford: Plymouth's Rock • 978-1-62486-092-8
Ernest Shackleton: Going South • 978-1-62486-093-5
Benjamin Rush: The Common Good • 978-1-62486-123-9
Dwight Eisenhower: Supreme Commander • 978-1-62486-142-0
Frederick Douglass: The Right to Dignity • 978-1-62486-151-2

Available in paperback, e-book, and audiobook formats.
Unit Study Curriculum Guides are available for many biographies.
www.YWAMpublishing.com